T0369999

THE
ANCIENT
WISDOM
OF
BASEBALL

Lessons for Life from
Homer's ODYSSEY to
the World Series

CHRISTIAN SHEPPARD

GREENLEAF
BOOK GROUP PRESS

Published by Greenleaf Book Group Press
Austin, Texas
www.gbgpress.com

Distributed by Greenleaf Book Group

For ordering information or special discounts for bulk purchases, please contact Greenleaf Book Group at PO Box 91869, Austin, TX 78709, 512.891.6100.

Design and composition by Greenleaf Book Group and Chase Quarterman
Cover design by Greenleaf Book Group and Chase Quarterman

The photograph of the Chicago White Stockings with the Great Sphinx of Giza, 1889, was obtained from the digital collection of the New York Public Library. The creator and copyright status are unknown.

Publisher's Cataloging-in-Publication data is available.

Print ISBN: 979-8-88645-304-1

eBook ISBN: 979-8-88645-305-8

To offset the number of trees consumed in the printing of our books, Greenleaf donates a portion of the proceeds from each printing to the Arbor Day Foundation. Greenleaf Book Group has replaced over 50,000 trees since 2007.

Printed in the United States of America on acid-free paper

25 26 27 28 29 30 31 32   10 9 8 7 6 5 4 3 2 1

First Edition

To Hille

CONTENTS

The Chicago White Stockings (later called the Cubs) with the Great Sphinx of Giza, 1889.[1]

PREGAME

My home ballpark, Wrigley Field, was built in 1914 by a chewing gum magnate upon the lot of a former seminary. Where identically dark-robed young men once gathered in silence to pray, now identically white-clad young men in blue caps, some in blue knee socks, gather to play a game. The pattern of Wrigley's girder work has a late-antebellum feel. From the outside it looks like a giant green-painted Mississippi riverboat somehow beached in the middle of the city. A national landmark, recognized by the American Institute of Architects as one of the hundred most-admired buildings in the country (the only sporting venue on the list), Wrigley is the most beloved landmark in Chicago. Airplanes flying over tilt their wings to give passengers a glimpse of its rough dirt diamond set inside its hexagonal emerald expanse.

Wrigley Field is not officially recognized as "sacred" by any traditional religious organization. Indeed, earnest sanctimony profanes the place's real magic. "Wrigley Field is my church," I intone in all piety, chewing a peanut, tossing the shell under my pew.

Yet folk use the old park to mark their lives' important moments. People make the pilgrimage from all over the country to see a game at Wrigley just once in their lifetime after years of cheering for the Cubs on TV. In a season, you'll see marriage proposals. When the park is open for tours, wedding parties wait to have their pictures taken. White bridal gowns look stunning against the vintage green seats and scoreboard. At every game, babies are held up along with hand-made signs announcing to all, "This is my first Cubs game." Old timers come to the park early and reminisce about past seasons and fellow fans no longer living. Newspaper obituaries deem it important enough to mention that the dearly departed was a lifelong Cubs fan. Some have even been caught surreptitiously dispersing cremated remains over the outfield wall, ashes sprinkling down onto the warning track dirt. From birth to mating to death, the stages of human life are marked at the park.

Most movingly, I witnessed a local soldier returned from Iraq, where a roadside bomb had robbed him of both legs and an arm. He hobbled on prosthetic legs out toward the pitcher's mound to (as was announced) fulfill his childhood dream of throwing out the first pitch at Wrigley. Out on the field, he fell to his knees. All forty thousand people gasped, thinking his artificial limbs had failed him, until it was clear he was kissing the earth in front of the pitcher's mound. Back up, he delivered a strike to the cheers and tears of the fans standing in recognition of the significance of the moment.

The veneration of generations has sanctified Wrigley Field as a place that is, well, sacred. But it emanates an odd sort of holiness. Best memories and imaginings, the famous field of dreams is also filled with boos and booze. If the ballpark is in some way a sacred place, it is always also unapologetically profane. I may be the only one to wonder aloud how what is, after all, only a game works for me better than any religion, but I do not feel alone.

·········

My daughter, Cecilia, was born in the spring of 1999. That year the Cubs would win sixty-seven games and lose ninety-five, finishing last in the National League Central. Yet in the maternity ward, watching the ball game with the sound off while my wife slept, whispering my own play-by-play as a lullaby for the napping newborn in my arms, I was blissfully ignorant of my team's fate.

There was a lot I didn't know.

....

"How are you going to raise her?"

The question came whispering from the shadows of the doorway. It was followed by a soft cough, then a slender figure clad in all black. This was Swift Hall, the Divinity School of the University of Chicago, the Department of Religion, a Gothic building of gray stone, part castle, part chapel, high-arched windows of leaded glass, slate roof framed with battlements and peaked by crosses. From the cornices, carved gargoyles grinned down. I was a student here and had just been steering the old-fashioned perambulator containing my infant daughter down the front stoop when I heard the question. I stopped.

The figure's face was pretty but pale. A glowing cigarette hung from her lips. Smoke rose from her nostrils as the question hung in the air between us. *How are you going to raise her?* Another long toke while her dark eyes slid to assess the small creature, my baby daughter, not much larger than one of the crows cawing in the just-budding tree limbs above us.

I recognized my questioner, a fellow graduate student outside in the cool air, slaking a craving for nicotine. Since the time of Hamlet and Horatio, the fashion for university students has been all black, especially those studying religion. She had not startled me. Nor was I puzzled by the question. "Her" referred to my baby. "How" meant morally, religiously, spiritually, philosophically:

What was I going to tell my daughter about heaven, hell, God, the devil, birth, rebirth, karma, nirvana, sin, salvation, eternal damnation, right, wrong, ethics—in other words, what was I going to teach her about how to live?

I was not taken aback by such a personal and prying question. Anywhere else it would have been an odd, if not downright rude, thing to ask. But Swift Hall was a place to question moral and metaphysical claims, to study and scrutinize worldviews and ways of life. Here the proverbial "devil's advocate" hung out, always ready to test biases and to tempt believers with doubt.

Though the question had been posed with cool nonchalance, it had been seriously put. It was the question that made me stop.

How to live is an ancient question, one that haunts human civilization's beginnings. Its earliest formulation may be the riddle of the sphinx. According to myth, the sphinx was a strange creature, half beautiful woman and half ferocious lion. The sphinx tempted and terrorized. She embodied both what men desired and what they feared. Lurking in the wilderness just beyond the ancient city walls, she posed her fatally befuddling riddles. Those who failed to answer correctly, she devoured.

None answered correctly or escaped her clutches until Oedipus, a wandering orphan unsure of his own identity. Here is the riddle she asked him: "What walks on four legs in the morning, on two legs in the afternoon, and on three legs in the evening?"

Eyeing her claws, Oedipus stalled. "Oh, man," he said, but as he spoke these words, a flicker of apprehension washed across the sphinx's beautiful visage, and Oedipus intuited the answer. "Of course," he exclaimed. "Man! As a child, a human crawls on all fours; as an adult, walks upright on two legs; and in old age, a cane makes three." The sphinx withdrew, never to trouble the city again. Thus self-knowledge may vanquish temptation and terror.

Yet her riddle may have another meaning. The answer points to the fact that human beings, too, are strange creatures. Although not a mixture of species like the sphinx, we are beings whose identity is a mystery to ourselves, and we are always changing and growing (if only older). Who am I? Who are you? Why am I here? Why are you? What is our aim, our purpose? What is the meaning of life? How are you going to raise her? These questions preoccupy and puzzle. The myth of the sphinx teaches that a human is a being for whom life is a question, for whom life—from childhood through maturity to old age, from beginning to middle to end—is a riddle.

"How are you going to raise her?" is another way of asking the sphinx's riddle. "How to live?" is a question posed to us all. And whether we ponder the riddle or ignore it altogether, each of us answers with our life.[2]

....

At Swift Hall, I made a quick response. "I'm going to raise her a Cubs fan." Out of reflex, I parried the question with irony. Irony is even more fashionable among divinity students than black.

For many in modernity, irony is all we have.

I was raised Roman Catholic, taught by habit-wearing nuns and collared Jesuits. When I told the priests I was going to the University of Chicago rather than Holy Cross or Boston College, they crossed themselves and shook their heads as though sorry to see another soul lost to Lucifer. In college, just as the priests had feared, I stopped going to Mass. Yet I did go on to graduate school to study religion, to ask about life's meaning, to answer for myself the questions the Church had once answered for me.

"That's right," I said again. "I'm going to raise her a Cubs fan."

My questioner crushed her cigarette and turned, withdrawing within the mock-Gothic academy. The large oaken door with its squeaking iron hinges and loud clattering lock swung shut behind her. I gazed down at my daughter, thinking about what I had said. Cecilia smiled up at me.

I whispered, "Want to go to the ball game?"

She laughed.

I nodded. "Yes!"

MYTHS

The moon, nearly full, glows over Fenway Park. It's the 1975 World Series. The Cincinnati Reds lead the Boston Red Sox three games to two, with a chance to win it all tonight. Almost midnight, Game 6 is tied 6–6 in overtime, the bottom of the 12th inning.

Red Sox catcher #27 Carlton Fisk leads off. He stretches before he enters the batter's box, holding his bat high over his head. He purposefully blinks and then stares into the middle distance, preparing his eyes to see the ball. Then he shakes his head and yawns, sticking out his tongue. From his demeanor, you wouldn't know that thirty-five thousand avidly watching, anxiously chattering human beings surround him or that seventy-six million more are watching on TV. Fisk steps into the box. He does not take his usual slow practice swings. He simply raises his bat. Ready.

The first pitch from the Reds reliever is high, a curve that does not drop. Ball one. Fisk steps out of the batter's box, lets the bat swing once like a pendulum, and then steps back in.

Now a fastball down and low. Actually, not that fast and down the middle. Fisk is all over it, so all over it that he's ahead of it. A loud knock sends it high and far but hooking left, seemingly foul, a white speck disappearing in the distant dark. Then with a discernible dong, the ball tolls off the tall yellow foul pole. The sound ignites a thunderous outburst from the surrounding thousands. A home run! The ball bounces to the grass near a Reds outfielder with his head hanging. The Boston fans scream, clap, stomp. Cheers rain down. As Fisk rounds the bases, the fans rush onto the field. He has to shoulder block a man trying to hug him along the third-base line. On his way to the dugout to escape the adoring throng, Fisk makes sure to step on home plate. Sox win!

THE SAME STORY BUT DIFFERENT

I've been remembering, replaying, and reflecting upon Fisk's home run, off and on, ever since I first witnessed it happen. I was seven years old, one of those seventy-six million watching on television, more than a third of the total US population at the time. I stayed up past my bedtime. When I woke up the next morning, it all seemed like a dream.

Ever since, I've enjoyed recurring flashbacks of momentary euphoria, recalling that scene at Fenway. Not just when I visit the park and look up at the left field pole. Fisk at the plate is one of my earliest and happiest memories. I will never forget it. I will never get tired of recalling it. And yet, for the longest time, I failed to grasp the story's meaning. I never got the point or even knew there was a point to get.

Before explaining further, let me tell the same story again, or at least another version of it. I will just change some of the details: the where, when, who, and what. The how and the why will stay the same. The story will have the same plot and make the same point.

More than three millennia before Carlton Fisk, the Greek hero Odysseus returns to his home island of Ithaca in the Ionian Sea after twenty years away.[1] Ten years he'd been lost at sea. Before that, he had been ten years at war in Troy. Odysseus returns home not in triumph but disguised as a beggar. You see, his house is filled with "guests," rivals who, during his long absence, have sought to seduce his queen, murder his only son and heir, and usurp his throne. (Odysseus' son Telemachus loathes these suitors—imagine 108 drunken bullies every day for your entire teenage years, inviting themselves over, emptying your fridge and pantry, pushing you around, and bragging about how they're going to marry your mom.) Odysseus' loyal wife, Penelope, as wily as she is lovely, has put off her rude suitors' advances season after season with excuses and ruses. But now they threaten to riot, and she is reduced to one final ploy.

Penelope has her husband's great bow brought into the hall and has twelve metal axe heads set up in a long row. Penelope invites everyone to try to string Odysseus' bow and shoot an arrow through the arrayed handle holes in the axe heads. The first to do so, she says, may marry her.

Suitors push one another out of the way to try, but none can even bend the bow to string it. Then Odysseus, anonymous in his filthy rags, steps forward. The suitors mock and jeer—hah, look at the old bum!—until with one swift motion, he bends the bow, hooks the string, and stretches it taut. Odysseus plucks the string once: Twang! The room goes hush as he nocks an arrow, draws, and sends it straight through all the axe holes and right into the center of the target.

Odysseus lets his disguise fall away so all may see that the hero has come home. Zeus, the king of the gods, hurls down a lightning bolt to punctuate the dramatic moment and signal his approval. The suitors shudder. Odysseus smiles, nocks another arrow, and sets about taking back his kingdom.

When moments later the ghost of the first slain suitor arrives in Hades, an arrow awkwardly still sticking through his neck, he retells this story of Odysseus' homecoming. The ghost of Agamemnon, Odysseus' old commander at Troy, the great king of kings—who was murdered by his disloyal wife's lover—shouts for all in Hades to hear: "Happy Odysseus!"[2] Indeed the final triumph of Odysseus will be celebrated for centuries as the archetypal happy ending to the hero's journey.

A DIFFERENT STORY BUT THE SAME

Carlton Fisk steps to the plate. Odysseus draws his bow. Two scenes separated by thousands of miles and thousands of years both present the same dramatic climax. A hero takes his chance to prove his excellence. He succeeds. Zeus illuminates the moment with lightning. The chorus of the crowd thunderously applauds. The hero has come home. Happiness ensues. Both stories show virtuosity rewarded with victory and joy.

Every baseball game, if viewed from the right angle, reenacts an ancient myth.

At the origins of Western civilization is Homer's epic poetry, stories of the fall of Troy, Achilles' wrath, and Odysseus' incredible journey home. When the first philosophers contemplated the good life, they talked about the virtues of Homer's heroes. Baseball also offers heroes whose actions point to life's ultimate purpose and promise: virtue and victory, or as we say today, excellence, success, and happiness.

A MEDIEVAL CHILDHOOD

I was raised in Irish Boston. I was taught by abusive nuns and inquisitive, ironical Jesuits. I was taught well, but not to question for myself. Rather I was raised to repeat a prescribed answer. God had revealed the answer in scripture, and the Church existed to interpret it. As a Catholic, all questions were asked and answered for me. Exemplary is the sixth question of the opening lesson of the Baltimore Catechism, once the official instruction manual for American Catholics:

Q: Why did God make you?

A: God made me to know Him, to love Him, and
to serve Him in this world, and to be happy with
Him for ever in heaven.

The Catechism claims to answer all of life's most important questions. To doubt its answers would be impious. To question, impertinent. But as a child, it never occurred to me to doubt or to question. It seemed to me that God had ordered the world perfectly. He—capital "H"—would reward goodness just as He would punish evil. If not here and now, then hereafter in heaven.

Meanwhile, every weekday morning, every child in my parish walked to the same school. Our Lady of the Presentation School stood near Our Lady of the Presentation Church, where on Sunday mornings, every family in my parish walked to attend the same Mass. We all stood, sat, and kneeled together. Together we all sang, recited, and prayed:

As it was in the beginning, is now, and ever shall be, world without end.

Amen.

"Amen" is Hebrew for "I believe." I didn't know this translation as a kid. I did not even know I was speaking Hebrew. To me *Amen* was just what you said at the end of every prayer, just like in old Westerns when they say "Stop" at the end of every line of a telegram. I didn't know what I was saying. Nevertheless I did believe. I believed the world would always be as it always was, Glory Be to the Father and to the Son and to the Holy Spirit. I crossed myself unselfconsciously, uncritically—believing in God more than gravity—in my thoughts and in my words and in my heart.

BAPTIZED IN THE CHURCH OF BASEBALL

I was also quite devoted to baseball. With my whole soul, I believed in the Red Sox. I went to Fenway Park for a half dozen games a season with my father or my grandfather. I gorged myself on Fenway Franks and stared beyond the Green Monster at the triangular Citgo sign glowing in the distance like some Pythagorean epiphany. I was present to witness the history of Carl Yastrzemski's 3,000th career hit.

Fenway, like Wrigley Field, is an old-time park in the middle of a busy city. Both places are beloved, dare I say, sacred places for devoted fans. (Of course, similar sentiments may be overheard at Chavez Ravine in Los Angeles, at New York's Yankee Stadium, in the brutalist concrete colosseum where the Toronto Blue Jays play, even in the newer Major League stadiums that resemble the misbegotten love children of amusement parks and strip malls. Wherever baseball memories and imaginings intermingle, an aura of significance arises.)

In my boyhood, the primary importance of periodically visiting Fenway Park was to reassure myself of its reality. Fenway was where the games that preoccupied my imagination all summer long were actually played. Every evening, I watched games on television until bedtime, then read the final score and corrected standings in the paper the next morning. My buddies and I replayed the games with our Wiffle bat and ball in the slower-trafficked streets of the neighborhood. I followed players' stats on the cards I collected, studied, and swapped. Baseball cards were our currency. I can no longer remember every player on that 1970s team roster. I do recall pitchers Luis Tiant and Bill "Spaceman" Lee, outfielders Jim Rice, Dwight Evans, Fred Lynn, Rico Petrocelli, Carl Yastrzemski, and the manager Don "Popeye" Zimmer, who in later years would manage the Cubs.

I was a Red Sox fan, that is, until the Red Sox betrayed me. In the spring of 1981, the Fenway front office committed the unforgivable sin of not re-signing my favorite player, all-star catcher #27 Carlton Fisk. To the then eleven-year-old backup backstop for the Oak Square Orioles, letting Fisk go undermined the institution of baseball altogether. This is an overreaction, to be sure, but even as a boy, I was a bit of a fanatic. When I believed in something, I believed with zealous passion. So I had been brought up. Any crack in the facade of my faith risked revealing any faults in the foundation. Imagine what other disillusionments awaited such an earnest, credulous child?

To this day I cannot understand how the Red Sox could let Fisk go.

A season or so earlier, I had composed a book report on *Fisk of Fenway Park: New England's Favorite Catcher* (1976) by Robert B. Jackson. For my English teacher, Sister Mary Anne, I recounted Fisk's athletic virtues and heroic deeds. A New Hampshire country boy, Fisk played the game right because he played it hard. Sometimes he played it too hard for his own health. He broke his arm, nose, fingers, and legs. He wasn't injury-prone. Fisk sacrificed his body to win. He was a martyr, Sister Mary Anne might say. I would say he was a hero. Every play at the plate, he was ready to take the collision and make the tag. He was also ready, if conscience required, to fist fight afterward.

And, of course, Fisk was the hero of that mythic drama, the 1975 World Series versus Cincinnati's "Big Red Machine" of Johnny Bench, Joe Morgan, mighty George Foster, and fiery Pete Rose. In my report, I told of the midnight home run Fisk hit to tie the Series 3–3. That ball tolling off the left field pole reverberated in my imagination no less than the American revolutionary "shot heard 'round the world" from the battlefield of Lexington and Concord. (Perhaps the defeated Pete Rose said it best: "Wasn't that the greatest game you've ever seen? Wasn't it fun?"[3])

When the Reds came back to beat the Red Sox in Game 7, it only made the story of the World Series more poignant. Victory eluded us, yes, but our Sox had fought gloriously. What we lost in a happy ending, we gained in laconic dignity.

"YANKEES SUCK" AND OTHER UNIVERSAL TRUTHS

Red Sox fans had to be connoisseurs of "laconic dignity." Our dignity existed in contrast to the grandeur of the ever-triumphant New York Yankees, tastefully understated in their classic classy pinstriped uniforms. On their backs, only numbers. No need for names. Everyone recognized Yankees players. They were always on national television. I picture an iconic Yankee, leaning on a bat, fist on jutted hip—the insouciant superiority embodied by Joe DiMaggio and, later, Derek Jeter.

My buddies and I didn't follow other teams in person or on the radio, but only through our card collecting and games against the Red Sox. Then at season's end, we settled down to watch the World Series, the grandest of events every autumn. We put aside our parochial sports interests each October in order to witness history. We were patriotic Americans, after all. But watching the World Series most often meant watching our American League East rivals, the Yankees.

It is a truth universally acknowledged, in New England if not elsewhere, that the Yankees suck. "Yankees suck" is Hebrew for "Yankees suck," as it is in every language spoken in the back streets of Boston. Pride in the Red Sox is balanced by prejudice against the Yankees. The goddess Fortuna mocked Boston as much as She doted on New York. The 1975 Red Sox World Series loss to the Reds was followed in 1976 by the Yankees facing (and losing—yay!) to the Reds. But again, in 1977, the Yankees won the Pennant and then went to the championship series, this time against the Los Angeles Dodgers. In that series, Yankees slugger Reggie Jackson accomplished something incredible.

Jackson was a husky fellow with a serious grown-up 1970s mustache. He had just come to the Yankees from the Oakland A's with a high salary and much braggadocio. Jackson had been known to say, "If I played in New York, they'd name a candy bar after me." Now he was in New York. And the Reggie candy bar soon followed: a massive mess of chocolate, nuts, and caramel that my friends and I all agreed was delicious.

Now on October 18, 1977, in Game 6 of the World Series, Reggie hit three home runs off three first pitches from three different pitchers. His first at bat, he walks. The first pitch in his second at bat, he shoots into the right field bleachers. His next at bat, he faces a new pitcher, whose first pitch he hits into the same roiling sea of screaming Yankees fans in right. It is like instant replay. His third homer, in my memory, forever earned him the audacious moniker "Mr. October."

My friends and I each separately watched the game on television, each saw it with his own eyes. I went with my father to my grandfather's house. My uncles pulled the TV out onto the back porch to be nearer the hot dogs grilling on the backyard hibachi. We were all quiet, listening to Howard Cosell's strange, stilted elocution, his elaborate diction, his hypnotic hyperbole. Some of my friends watched in living color. I saw it in grainy, jumpy black-and-white. After the game, my grandfather turned off the television, my uncles went inside. My father and I walked two blocks home under blinking streetlights and indifferently staring stars. A distant horn beeped in the lonely night. My father said, "Jackson is a great player."

I nodded and muttered, "Yankees suck."

The next day my friends and I repeated the story to one another, took turns telling it again, adding details. I can still see in my mind Jackson's heroic physique as he took his third victory lap around the bases against the classical columns of old Yankee Stadium. The screaming thousands in the imperial metropolis called for him to bow. When he stepped from the dugout in his batting helmet and large glasses, he seemed like a gladiator saluting the crowd, his signature long sleeves looking like armor.

The third pitcher he had faced had been a knuckleballer. We related the tale in whispers. The pitch floats and darts like a drunken fairy, like dying Tinkerbell. The point is that when Jackson hits it, the power is all his own. The last home run goes the farthest. Is it 450 or 475 feet? It has to be almost 500 feet! It bounces into the tar-black batter's eye beyond center field. A shot straight into the astonished, staring eye of an Olympian god. Cosell's adjectives will echo in our minds: "Colossal." "A Monster." "What a blow!" "Splendid!" As if Reggie is David defeating Goliath. When, in fact, he is a giant among an entire New York team of titans.

We debated Reggie's achievement for years. Someone would comment that only one other player had ever accomplished such a feat. We all nodded. All knew: "Babe Ruth." Then we all shook our heads. We all also knew that once upon a time, the Red Sox had traded Ruth for money, filthy lucre, for an amount that in biblical silver must have been identical to the salary Judas had been paid to betray Jesus. Ruth had accomplished the feat twice, actually hitting three homers in two different World Series games, someone interjected, as if this might diminish Jackson's accomplishment. But did Ruth ever do it on three first pitches? I like Reggie's candy bar better, another kid said. Then someone else spoke up and pointed out the obvious unbearable truth: both Ruth and Reggie were Yankees. We all shook our heads, muttering in unison: "Yankees suck."

FROM HOMER TO HOMERS

Honesty required that one admit admiration for Reggie Jackson. But Carlton Fisk was my favorite player. I still can't forget Fisk's stance at the plate. Legs a little wide, slightly bent over, he swept the bat forward through the zone twice, like two practice strokes of an axe before taking a first fresh hard cut into a living tree. Still now when I stand waiting (for an elevator or at the bus stop), I catch myself mimicking Fisk. And my imaginary hits are like his were: line drives shot from a cannon.

I contemplated in Fisk what I now know to call "ancient virtues": courage, prudence, and temperance. These ancient virtues are the founding values of classical civilization. They underlie Greco-Roman mythology, are preserved in the tradition of epic literature begun by Homer, and are expounded in the philosophical tradition started in ancient Athens by Socrates. And these same heroic virtues can be recovered by contemplating the game of baseball. I just didn't know it when I was seven years old, or when I was eleven, or even when I was thirty-one. I did not see the meaning and morals dramatized by baseball. I did not recognize that each and every game plays out, like a ritual reenactment, a mythic story.

Fisk showed the courage to stand in there and make the tag. A catcher, of course, needs prudence, practical smarts, almost as much as a pitcher to call a game behind the plate. As well as any player, Fisk had the cool temperance required to compete at the big league level for an entire season. Fisk's usual ballplayer's controlled temper could be appreciated that much more when, for a moment, he would lose it, for example, fighting with some of the Cincinnati Reds. I would not have been able to enumerate all of Fisk's virtues for Sister Mary Anne, nor could I have traced the pedigree of these characteristics back to classical myth. I would never have dared to conceive of, much less confess, baseball as a substitute for religion. Yet then, in the simpler times of childhood, the mere example of a hero's exploits and the glory of his story were enough for emulation and the pursuit of excellence in your own life.

How could the Red Sox have let such a player go? It boggled my mind. At the time, of course, I did not appreciate this lesson in life's tragic indifference or in fortune's mocking fickleness. It just broke my heart and left me bitter. The Red Sox front office had dismayed me in a way that even the sucking Yankees had never done. To protest Fisk's departure, I stopped playing baseball myself, I stopped following the Red Sox. I even stopped watching the World Series.

And perhaps because of the absence of baseball from my life, when the simple faith of my youth fell away, I was left questioning the meaning of life, why we are here, how we should live. The blind belief of my childhood was gone. Baseball meant little to me. Church even less. It was when I came to Chicago's South Side for college that I began to follow the game again. During my first spring there, I went to old Comiskey Park, where Fisk (now #72) played behind the plate for the Chicago White Sox. For my nineteenth birthday, my new girlfriend surprised me with tickets. Perhaps this last sight of my hobbled childhood hero helped open my mind again to the game. It certainly opened my heart to that girl. We never stopped dating until we got married. She went into law; I to graduate school. We moved to the North Side, became Cubs fans, and had a baby, Cecilia.

There was a lot I didn't know. But was I really going to raise my baby daughter a Cubs fan?

I had been raised to fear a God I now no longer believed in. So how was I to raise my own child? After all of my academic study, I had no answer. I did not know what I would tell her about God, the devil, good, evil, Vishnu, Buddha, love, nature, death or the soul, or the meaning of life. Was I now so confused or so cynical that all I had to impart were my doubts?

I did have plenty of doubts. These I could readily express. But looking down at my baby smiling up at me, my questions were no longer academic. My feelings were beyond questioning. I felt love, fatherly love. I knew I wanted her to be happy.

I could not tell her something I did not believe myself. I couldn't raise her to live other than by my own example. The question of how to raise her put into question how I ought to live. It was a question I could no longer be content to leave unanswered. How could I help her be happy? Should I take her to Mass, or meditate with her upon the sayings of the Zen masters or the desert fathers, or something else, or nothing else?

Yet nothing is something. My wife had been raised nothing by her loving parents, an atheistic rocket scientist and a universally tolerant social worker, and she knew no better what to tell our child. She was never raised with any faith and was not troubled by doubts. To my questions, she simply shrugged and, whispering softly over the sleeping child in her arms, said, "I dunno, you're the one getting the PhD in religion."

Fast-forward to Cecilia at one year old. It's just her and me, wandering the North Side of Chicago. I bring a book along, usually a dog-eared copy of Homer's *Odyssey*, which I am teaching in the University of Chicago's "Great Books" program. A radio rides under the carriage. From AM 720 WGN, the voices of Pat Hughes and Ron Santo announce the Cubs game. Hughes's mellifluous voice fluently narrates the play-by-play. Santo groans, moans, and screams, a cranky old horn expressing all the emotions of any given moment of the game. Sometimes, fleeing static, I cross the street or turn a corner in search of better reception. I find myself walking faster or slower depending upon the inning's action. Not surprisingly, as the weather gets a little warmer, Cecilia and I find ourselves approaching Wrigley Field. We can hear the crowd cheering from blocks away.

We enter under the big red Jazz-Age sign at the corner of Clark and Addison. Tickets checked, we're through the turnstile and into shadows. The ground is slick and sticky. The crowd is thick and loud. Vendors hawk programs, snacks, and beverages. Smell the beer, onions grilling, popcorn. Take it in, all the cramp and damp, darkness and noise. Soon we'll savor the contrast. With Cecilia on one arm and her diaper bag and blankets on the other, I cut through the throng and head up the stairs. Feel the bracing breeze. Springtime in Chicago feels like winter most anywhere else, but the blue sky promises better weather. At the top step, we find ourselves right behind home plate, with the dirt diamond before us and, spreading beyond, green grass and budding ivy.

Players sprint across the outfield. Others stretch and play catch. The starters are warming up in the pens. Like toy pieces unpacked from the box before play begins, we see the game in fragments, snapshots, highlights. All has the pastoral sense of summer ball, of games remembered from past seasons, not necessarily any particular player or play but just what you think about when you think about baseball: hitting, catching, throwing . . .

. . . .

When Homer sang of Odysseus stringing his great bow hundreds of years before, he compared the first twang of the bowstring to the plucking of a string on his own musical instrument, the lyre. He used the lyre to bring the mythic moment into the imaginations of his listeners. Homer's listeners heard the hero's bow exactly as they heard the poet's lyre. The old blind singer conjured the hero to be present among them, so that way back then seemed like right here now, as if the famous hero stood before them.

An accident of television broadcasting caused something similar to occur during Fisk's mythic moment. Caught up in the excitement of the game, one of the NBC camera operators failed to follow the ball and instead let his lens linger on Fisk, capturing for all to see the player's reaction. Fisk hopped sideways down the first-base line, gesturing with both arms, begging for the ball to stay fair. Then—home run!—he leapt into the air. In his gestures of supplication and jubilation, you could see that Fisk was also a fan. He shared our joy. The crowd rushing onto the field in Fenway only fulfilled this sense. Our hero was one of us. He was like you, like me, so happy.

When virtue turns to victory, when excellence becomes success, the hero's example imprints itself upon your psyche, just as it is etched into our collective memory. The image of Odysseus drawing his bow can be seen decorating countless Grecian urns. I've seen this scene carved in pale alabaster on a funerary urn, dug up from the necropolis, the city of the dead, of Volterra in Tuscany. Some ancient Etruscan savored Odysseus' victory enough to be buried with its image.

Similarly, the photo of Fisk with hands raised, when supplication turned to jubilation, is displayed at the Baseball Hall of Fame in Cooperstown, New York, at the Louisville Slugger Factory in Kentucky, and still, nearly fifty years later, in barrooms and restaurants all over New England. It is an indelible image in the minds of Red Sox fans. Against a background of continual consternation (and only recent success), Fisk's arms aloft are like "Winged Victory."

How to live? This is a question we each must answer. In our thoughts and in our words and in our deeds, we answer. We answer in how we think, act, and react, in how we cooperate and compete with one another, and in how we coordinate ourselves emotionally and intellectually with society and nature. Yes, we must each answer the question of how to live for ourselves and with our lives, but how?

Pointing toward the answer are Homer's myths and the games played at the ballpark.

My baby daughter, Cecilia, points up to the sky. What does she see? A baseball flying by! Follow the ball's trajectory, like following an arrow shot from the bow of Odysseus, it will lead you toward an answer.

2ND INNING

VIRTUE

I was in my first year of college when I went to Wrigley Field for the first time. We sat in the right field bleachers overlooking #8 Andre Dawson, "The Hawk." I don't remember much from that first game. Who knows the score or who won or even who the Cubs were playing! It was just another day game in another losing season in nearly a century of defeat and disappointment for a team whose record any sensible baseball fan would just as soon forget. But, I tell you, I'll never forget the first time I saw Dawson in action. It was a play not only worth remembering, but worth thinking and rethinking about, worthy of what the ancient philosophers called "contemplation."

After an already long career, Dawson is a man of immense athletic talent, honed skill, and competitive spirit, but he was cursed with chronic injuries. It was rumored his knees were ruined playing on artificial turf in Montreal. In 1987, his year of free agency, the story goes, he wanted to play for the Cubs, so instead of negotiating, he signed a blank contract, telling management to fill in whatever salary they thought fair.

In his first season with the Cubs, he hits 49 homers, bats in 137 runs, and is the National League's Most Valuable Player. He is the only player with a last-place team ever to win the award. Against a background of dim, unmemorable mediocrity, the

brilliance of Dawson's excellence gleams brighter. Even now looking back on him with his 70s' Jheri curls, he resembles an electric
blues guitarist rather than a hero (although many of my heroes
are electric guitarists). He walks pigeon-toed and top heavy. His
deeply creased face seems to brood beneath his cheery Cubby-
blue cap. He remains a distinctly anomalous figure against the
leafy-green background.

....

I remember clearly: there is a runner on first base when the ball
is hit into the right field corner. It strikes off the ivy—a single
leaf flutters down—and it bounces to the brick sidewall. The ball
then rolls away along the dirt trench back toward the bullpen. The
runner, glancing once over his shoulder to see old Andre stooped
and chasing after it, decides to head for home.

BALL AS SPHERE

Let us for a moment, while the Hawk looks for it, think about the
ball itself. What is a baseball? Two large, peanut-shaped pieces
of bleached cowhide stitched together with oxblood red twine.
Inside are 219 yards of yarn—enough to stretch from first to second to third to home and then all the way out to Dawson near
Wrigley's right field wall—this twine is wound tightly around a
corked rubber ball. The rubber is from the Amazonian jungle,
where the jaguars still roam. Once upon a time in some remote
places, they used fish eyes at the core of the ball, but now they use
cork. Inside the cork are a lot of little holes. Inside the little holes
is nothing. We can go no further, though I feel we have not quite
gotten to the true center or significance of the ball.

Geometrically speaking, a ball is a sphere. Ancient philosophers studied geometry in order to perfect their powers of reasoning. In ancient Alexandria in Egypt, the philosopher Euclid contemplated the sphere. Euclid's *Elements*, the first geometry textbook, says: "When a semicircle with fixed diameter is carried round and restored again to the same position from which it began to be moved, the figure so comprehended is a sphere."[1] This definition of the sphere holds as true for our humble baseball as it does for the sun itself. Yet a perfect sphere exists nowhere but in our minds. The philosopher's sphere is only an intellectual concept abstracted in the imagination from all the balls rolling around in the real world, including those of stitched leather called baseballs.

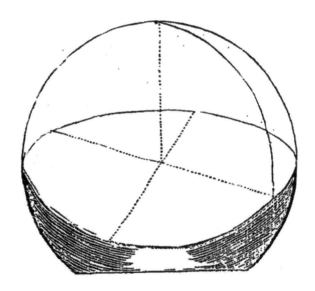

Any size sphere presents perfect symmetry.[2]

BALL AS WEAPON

A baseball's primary purpose, however, is not contemplation. Like the game from which it takes its name, a baseball is beautifully, symmetrically well-proportioned for action, for playing. Its proportions are human. As the handle of a bat is honed to be swung, the ball is sized and shaped for a hand of four parallel digits and an opposable thumb. Hold a baseball in your hand and you can feel what it is for. The ball is made to be thrown.

This meaning of the ball is corroborated by archaeology. Ball games began with the beginning of the city. We can look back to the ancient Mediterranean coast for the foundation of the first cities and the evolution of human beings into true social animals. Early humans were pastoral beings. We nomads wandered the plains of the Near East, hunting gazelle, sheep, goats, and cattle. We gathered fruits, nuts, cereal, and wild grasses.

About fourteen thousand years ago, we began to build stone houses and figure out how to farm. In a few millennia, as many as eight thousand people had created a permanent community in Catalhöyük, Turkey, not far from legendary Troy. (For point of comparison, that's about as many people as sit on any given game day in the bleachers at Wrigley and the rooftops beyond.) Found among these ruins of this earliest city, aside from the carved figurines of the original mother goddesses, were many clay balls. Cecilia and I saw these artifacts for ourselves at the University of Chicago's museum of archaeology, the Institute for the Study of Ancient Cultures (where, by the way, Indiana Jones studied for his PhD). The dull clay balls—do they belong in a museum?—seemed almost suspicious in their simplicity, displayed alongside the golden treasures of Egypt and colossal imperial statuary of Babylon. Researchers cannot be sure what these balls were for. They are the size of baseballs, meaning they are perfect for fitting into the human hand, perfect for throwing. Some speculate that the clay balls were used as toys or for a game. Others think the balls were used in warfare. Sports may have their origin as preparation for war. A ball recalls the original missile weapons of our primitive ancestors, just as the bat recalls our original bludgeons. And like a bat, a baseball can serve as a weapon. (Never start a snowball fight with Nolan Ryan!)

BALL AS BALL

Just as conflict may become competition, a projectile can be adapted for play. Here we discern the ball's true purpose and meaning. So now see the ball. Put aside its abstract definition and original purpose. Focus on one particular baseball, the one bouncing around the right field corner where our all-star out-fielder Andre "The Hawk" Dawson hurries, shuffling after it.

Oh, when Dawson catches up to the rolling ball, when he gets his grip on that elusive sphere, suddenly everything falls into place—the grass and the ivy, city and sky—when in one motion, Dawson turns and throws. Stepping forward, releasing the ball, Dawson, in his pinstripes, presents a schematic figure of dynamic action. The ball, the total focus of forty thousand fervid fans' attention, presents the trajectory of the Hawk's intention. I can still see it, like a bullet shot at the plate. Then it's there, the ball, arriving the moment just before the runner's cleats can touch home. The catcher has made the tag. The runner is "out!"

In the right field bleachers, we fans fawningly "salaam," arms outstretched, bowing deeply to Dawson. He does not crack a smile. He keeps his intense frown, the ballplayer's stoical expression. He refuses to gloat over the defeat of others. He is humble because he knows how much fortune plays in our victories as in our defeats. Had he been kept bending on aching knees, chasing for that elusive ball a fraction of a second longer, a run would have scored.

At that moment in the spring of 1988, when I first cheered for the Cubs, Cecilia was not even thought of (my wife and I had only been dating for a few months). When I recall Dawson's throw now, I recognize it as the intuition of an answer. I did not know then, just as Cecilia later does not know when she reaches up for a ball flying by high in the sky, that the graceful line it describes through blue air over green grass can answer the question I've been asking, the question she by her very birth has provoked: How to live?

Now I know: Dawson's throw embodies, exemplifies what the ancient poets and philosophers called *arête*—virtue, excellence. The question of life's meaning is a how-to question. On the one hand, a ball flies, bounces, rolls. So a ball represents chance and contingency. But on the other hand, a ball can be hit, caught, and thrown. So a ball—get a good grip on it—offers the opportunity for excellence.

Q: How should I raise her? How should we live?

A: Do everything in life as excellently as Andre
        Dawson threw that baseball.

HEY! HEY!

While my daughter and I watch the big leaguers play catch, I am reminded of Dawson's throw as well as of other great throws I have seen. In my youth, #24 Dwight "Dewey" Evans had a cannon in right at Fenway Park. Bo Jackson, oh Bo, for the Chicago White Sox. But before that, before his injury, just out of college, Bo was #16 for the Kansas City Royals. What an arm!

A legendary throw was made at the Polo Grounds in Manhattan during Game 1 of the 1954 World Series between the Cleveland Indians and the New York Giants, a play that is known as "The Catch." Top of the 8th inning, the game tied 2–2, two Indians are on base when slugger Vic Wertz hits one long and high into center. It's now estimated by sports scientists and scholars of "The Catch" that Wertz's well-struck ball traveled some 420 feet, a home run in most other Major League ballparks, but the center field lawn at the old Polo Grounds is vast, and the young Giants outfielder #24 Willie Mays is fast. Mays sprints directly beneath the soaring ball, catching it over his shoulders like a wide receiver pulling in a Hail Mary pass.

Jack "Hey, Hey" Brickhouse (the distinct voice of the Chicago Cubs from 1941–1981) calls the game that day for NBC Sports:

> "There's a long drive . . . way back in center
> field . . . way back, back, it is . . . caught by Willie
> Mays! Willie Mays just brought this crowd to its
> feet with a catch which must have been an optical
> illusion to a lot of people. Boy!"[3]

Yet Mays's "Catch" might just as well be known as "The Throw." Journalist Arnold Hano was at the Polo Grounds that day. He wrote one of the classics of baseball literature, *A Day in the Bleachers*, an entire book dedicated just to describing and reflecting upon the action on the field during that game. Hano devotes ten pages of dense prose to appreciating Mays's play. He explains that "the play was not finished with the catch":

The throw to second base was something else again.

Mays caught the ball, and then whirled and threw,
like some olden statue of a Greek javelin hurler,
his head twisted away to the left as his right arm
swept out and around. . . .

But the throw! What an astonishing throw, to
make all other throws ever before it . . . appear the
flings of teen-age girls. This was the throw of a
giant, the throw of a howitzer made human . . . .[4]

Mays's throw arrives in time to hold the Indians runners at
first and third, prevent them from scoring, keeping the game
knotted in a tie. The Giants would go on to win the game in extra
innings and sweep the World Series in three more games.

Hano cannot stop contemplating the meaning of Mays's feat:
"Making a great catch and whirling and throwing, before another
man would have been twenty feet from the ball. . . . Mays must
be regarded as off by himself, not merely *a* great ball player, but
the great ball player of our time."[5]

Such excellence inspires such reflections, calculations, evalu-
ations. Here is the origin of all bleacher and barroom arguments
about ranking best, greatest, most excellent players and plays.
An epiphany of excellence calls out for praise, appreciation, and
contemplation.

ENTER ODYSSEUS

Now I am reminded of another throw. Unlike my story of Andre
Dawson, which is a mere fragment of a personal memory, this

story is classic, deemed worth remembering for millennia. In Homer's epic the *Odyssey*, Odysseus—Sing me, oh Muse, of him for whom ever after all far-ranging journeys of discovery and adventure are named, he of the loyal son, the true wife, the re-won kingdom, Athena the goddess of wisdom's favorite—yes, that Odysseus, once upon a time made a great throw. It wasn't a baseball he threw, but a discus. Precisely when this throw occurred is uncertain. Homer composed his epic in the eighth century BCE, but he was recounting events that had occurred in pre-history, perhaps as far back as five centuries earlier, in other words, more than three thousand years before young Andre Dawson started playing Little League on a hot sandlot in South Miami, Florida. Like Dawson's throw and that by Willie Mays, the throw by Odysseus is a revelation of excellence.

As the blind poet Homer sings of it, Odysseus has lost his way home from destroyed Troy. After ten years of wandering, he washes ashore on the remote island kingdom of Phaeacia. Odysseus has no ship, no crew, no identification, no weapons, no money. He is exhausted, naked, bleeding, feeling old and cold. When the princess of the island and her maidens have a beach party within earshot of the pile of driftwood under which Odysseus sleeps, he makes his presence known. Odysseus has a way with words. Filthy and naked, he can still convince the princess to lend him some clothes and take him to the palace. He talks the queen into giving him a seat at the royal table. He speaks so well that the king welcomes him and invites him to stay. But all Odysseus wants is a bath, a bite, and a lift to his own home island of Ithaca. The hospitable islanders are happy to oblige.

While waiting for the ship to be prepared, the Phaeacians hold a banquet in honor of their mysterious guest. (Odysseus, out of caution, has not let slip his name.) Phaeacia is a utopia.

Its citizens are generous hosts, talented athletes, and fantastic dancers. Their court performers play the lyre beautifully and know all the classic bardic songs. During the celebration, one young islander—perhaps not so bright or so impressed by eloquent talk, or perhaps a little drunk (like a kid who's wandered in from a day in the bleachers at Wrigley after his first one-too-many beers)— challenges Odysseus to prove his worth in an athletic contest. The young man practically accuses Odysseus of being a coin-counting, conniving merchant with the slick tongue of a salesman. He can talk the talk, but can he walk the walk?

Odysseus strides onto the field where the young athletes are throwing the discus. He takes one up and lets it fly. Homer specifies that the discus Odysseus throws is much larger than all the others. Imagine a manhole cover flying over ducking heads. The umpire (the goddess Athena in disguise) declares that even a blind person could feel how far this throw has out-distanced the others. His spirit roused, Odysseus challenges all the youth of the island to any contest they choose: boxing, wrestling, spear-throwing, or archery. He boasts he was better with arrow and bow than all the heroes at Troy save the famed archer Philoctetes. He will defeat all challengers. Odysseus has dropped the first hint as to his true identity. He is one who fought at Troy! The events of the Trojan War are already legend-ary. This man had defeated (and destroyed) one of the world's greatest cities. The islanders are shocked into silence.

How to explain the full import of this moment?

ENTER ICHIRO

In 2001 we saw the arrival of a rookie for the Seattle Mariners who had already played nine seasons in Japan for the Orix Blue

Wave NPB (Nippon Professional Baseball). Ichiro Suzuki's reputation preceded him. He was a celebrity in his home country, referred to adoringly by his first name only, "Ichiro," like Elvis or Beyoncé. Some thought it presumptuous that his first name would appear on the back of his Mariners uniform. This short, wiry, quietly smiling fellow was rumored to be an extraordinary ballplayer, hitting for average and for power, speed on the base paths, and a great arm in the field. But the rumors were from Japan. In the spring of 2001, it was still uncertain what the Mariners had in their twenty-seven-year-old rookie.

On April 11, 2001, in the eighth game of the season, #51 Ichiro introduces himself to America. Ichiro does not start but is brought into the game in the 8th inning as a pinch hitter (he gets a hit) and then trots out to play right field. A few minutes later, when the Oakland A's Terrence Long—running from first base with a good jump on a slow bouncer into shallow right—turns for third, Ichiro charges the ball. He leans and scoops it smoothly into his mitt. Then without pause in his swift pace, he switches the ball to his bare hand and, with the full force of his forward stride, throws "a laser beam strike!"[6] to the lip of the third base bag, meeting Long at the end of his slide. "Out!"

Long hops up, wide-eyed and blinking at Ichiro, now squatting on his heels in right field. "It was going to take a perfect throw to get me," Long later says, "and it was a perfect throw."[7] A clip of Ichiro's "Throw" was played over and over again for the next week on ESPN's Sports Center. I feel like I watched the replay at least fifty times. The announcer's first words were the best words: "a laser beam strike!" It was thrown on a line, as a philosophical geometrician might define it, the shortest distance between two points. Although his reputation had preceded him, like Odysseus, Ichiro's virtuosity confirmed that he deserved his fame.

In 2001, Ichiro won Rookie of the Year as well as American League Most Valuable Player. He also won the most votes for the All-Star Game. In 2001, the Mariners would go 116–46, tying the 1906 Cubs record for the most wins in a regular season, although the Mariners would lose in the AL Championship Series to the Yankees ("Yankees suck" is Japanese for "Yankees suck"). Mariners' manager Lou Piniella said of his rookie right fielder: "This guy Suzuki, he hits, bunts, and steals. He scores before you know it. He sets the tone for the team. He's phenomenal."[8] Of course, this "guy Suzuki" would go on to win ten Gold Gloves, be voted ten times an All-Star, twice win MLB batting champion, set the record for most hits in a single season (262), set the record for consecutive 200-hit seasons (ten), and break Pete Rose's record for career hits (more than 4,367). And we've only scratched the surface of the excellence, the magnificence of Ichiro.

ALREADY FAMOUS

But even Ichiro's arrival in America cannot quite capture the surprise, shock, and awe of the revelation of Odysseus in Phaeacia. Who is this stranger who displays the abilities of a hero? Imagine if Ichiro were revealed to actually be Ty Cobb reborn! Maybe the Dalai Lama could certify the authenticity of his reincarnation. Odysseus was already a legend in his own time, an indisputable, universally recognized hero.

When the Phaeacian king bids him sit, to quell his fiery spirit by listening to some songs, Odysseus requests the ballad of the Trojan Horse. Of course the singer knows that instant classic. He strokes his lyre and sings of the parting "gift" the Greek army had left on the beach after apparently retreating: a giant horse made of wood. To make such a sculpture from timber required the skill of experienced shipbuilders. To conceive of such a trick required the cunning of a devious-minded genius such as Odysseus. He knew that the Trojans, renowned for their horsemanship and for their love of horses, could not resist dragging such a spectacular equine sculpture, a sign of their triumph, through their gates and into their city center.

At night, a squad of soldiers led by Odysseus climbed out from a hidden chamber inside the wooden horse's belly. They quietly unlocked the city gates and led the secretly returned Greek army to slaughter and enslave the Trojans and burn the city of Troy to the ground. After listening to this song, his own theme music, our hero reveals himself as Odysseus, son of Laertes. "My fame," he says, "ascends to heaven."[9] The Phaeacians, who have just witnessed his excellence throwing the discus, all nod. They believe it.

The Phaeacian king congratulates Odysseus on his *arête*, and so explains the meaning of Odysseus' throw. In so doing, he also explains the meaning of the throws of Dawson, Mays, and Ichiro. It is what I see in the players playing catch before the game. It is why we instinctively reach for a ball. It may even be present when Cecilia and I roll a ball back and forth to one another on the carpet in front of the cat.

ἀρετή

Arête is an ancient term, usually translated as "virtue." We must distinguish ancient virtue, however, from the now-common use of "virtue" to mean merely goody two-shoes, Pollyanna best intentions. Virtue ought to be associated with virtuosity. With being able to do things well: shoot an arrow, run up a sandy beach fully armored into the bronze teeth of an enemy phalanx, negotiate peace, deliver a speech, flatter a princess, solve a riddle, throw a discus or a baseball. The root of the English word "virtue" is the Latin *virtus*, meaning "manliness." The Romans thought it manly to be handy, to be able, to have ability. The Greek word *arête* can be traced back to Ares, the god of war. War for the Greeks was the crucible of competition, a game with lethal stakes where character was forged and virtue displayed. The best translation, then, is virtuosity, or the ability to do something well. Or more simply—excellence.

My own throwing arm is pretty weak. In Little League, I was moved in from the outfield, but not to pitch. I played catcher in part because my arm was only good enough to toss the ball back to the mound. I am no "howitzer made human." Not so for Cecilia. Her arm is terrific! She threw overhand from the beginning. She naturally stepped into it and followed through. By the time she was ten, her throws hit the mitt with a nice rifle crack. She might play catch in a dress, but never in her life has Cecilia "thrown like a girl."

From Odysseus' strong-arm throw (in a tunic, kind of like a dress), this moment of *arête*, his epic story follows. Odysseus reveals himself, tells his tale, goes back to Ithaca, and exercises all of his other virtues in order to win back his kingdom. This revelation of a hero's identity will become the fully elaborated myth, the story of his homecoming. Homer's *Iliad* is about destroying a kingdom. The *Odyssey* is about a long journey home to restore a kingdom. These are the stories Western civilization has been telling itself for three millennia.

Baseball can help us recover this essential sense of excellence. Every ball game tells once more the ancient story about virtue and victory that modern folk can witness with their own eyes. The throws of Dawson, Mays, and Ichiro, like Odysseus', answer the question of how to live: Know yourself, and let yourself be known, by your excellence.

COURAGE

"Don't be afraid of the ball!" This advice is repeated from behind every chain-link backstop in America. And with good reason. The same reason the person giving the advice is hiding behind a backstop. When a fast-traveling hard ball hits you (rather than you hitting it), you could be left injured, ugly, stupid, or even dead. Most often, though, getting hit by a pitch just really hurts.

"Pitching is the art of instilling fear," legendary ace #32 Sandy Koufax said.[1] So hitting requires steeled nerves to stand in there and take a swing. You'd have to be dumb not to be wary. Even the dimmest-witted designated hitter instinctively flinches from an "artful" pitcher's "chin music." The amygdala, the reptilian center of the brain concerned with survival, with fight and flight, detects the stone-like object hurtling toward us and suggests we step back. To drown out your tiny inner dinosaur's prudent suggestion, parents and coaches and teammates repeat, "Don't be afraid of the ball!" Hitting teaches courage.

Courage is the first of the traditional cardinal virtues, according to Aristotle. You may have lots of good ideas. You may have the best intentions. But without the courage to act, all the other virtues are worthless. Good ideas and best intentions, if never acted upon, are no better than ignorance or indifference. Only action actually accomplishes anything. And to act requires courage.

ANCIENT ACTION HERO

According to ancient tradition, the embodiment of courage was the hero Achilles. Achilles was naturally talented. Homer cannot mention his name without adding that he is fast. He is always "fleet-footed Achilles." And his talents were trained. His childhood tutor in the martial arts was the centaur Chiron, so the young hero was schooled in the ways of both beasts and men. For his virtuosity in killing, his enemies feared him as his allies revered him.

But Achilles represents courage not because he was a fine and ferocious fighter. Every hoplite who straps on his greaves before battle, just like every batter who steps into the batter's box, must be brave. The legend goes that Achilles, the mortal child of a goddess, was granted a unique choice. He could decide his fate, whether to live a long, peaceful life in the safety of obscurity or a life glorious in its excellence but cut short by violence. In other words, he could live a long life behind the backstop, or he could have a shining but short career and die in the batter's box. Achilles consciously chose what we all naturally fear: violent death.

Once Achilles chose, he was without fear. Once resolved, he never again hesitated. He was all action. Most other heroes, mortals like you or me, need to summon the courage to overcome our natural aversion to danger. Nike encourages us to "Just do it." We need encouragement. Not Achilles; he embodied courage. While everyone is still tying their laces, he is already done. He is off to the war at Troy, there to die, to fight fearlessly and skillfully so that he might be remembered forever.

Achilles' feats at Troy were made unforgettable by Homer's first great work, the founding epic of Western civilization, the *Iliad*.[2] It is said that there are two essential plots in literature: man goes on a trip and man comes to town. (Man goes on a trip is, of course, the *Odyssey*, Homer's other great work.) The *Iliad* is man comes to town. The town in question is Troy, a magnificent high-walled city on the far eastern coast of the Mediterranean in a region called Ilium. The man who came was Achilles and, with a little help from his fellow Greeks, especially Odysseus and his trick wooden horse, he destroyed the place. (Achilles was Godzilla; Troy, Tokyo.) Specifically, Achilles defeated the Trojan champion Hector in single combat before the eyes of both armies. Achilles' presence proved so intimidating that Hector, harkening to his amygdala, fled rather than face him. The Trojans watched and trembled as Achilles chased their champion three times all the way around their city walls. Being "fleet of foot," Achilles caught Hector. He killed him, then dragged his mutilated corpse behind his chariot as a macabre trophy. Although it would take Odysseus and his wooden horse to finally destroy Troy, the city's spirit was broken the day Achilles slew Hector.[3]

Once, Troy had been the epitome of ancient civilization, commerce, and culture. By the time the Greeks left, it was fit only as a subject for poetry and archaeology, to be sung of or dug up. Today you can still visit the glory that was Greece and the glamour that was Rome, but there's not even a ruin left to wander in or wonder at where Troy's lofty walls once stood. Homer's song of Achilles, the embodiment of courage, the foremost action hero, remains the incredibly beautiful, inspiring, and heartbreakingly tragic founding epic of Western civilization.

HONOR YOUR ENEMY

Another classical virtue (not a cardinal virtue such as courage but a virtue that nonetheless can help us better understand courage) is honoring one's foes. This is what today we call good sportsmanship.

Homer, who was Greek, concludes his *Iliad* by honoring the Trojan Prince Hector. Honoring your opponent's virtues and recognizing the worthiness of your foe complements the ancient ideal of competition. It is through competition in war, sports, politics, even in the arts, that our virtues are cultivated and our characters forged. Only if your enemy is worthy will your victory be worthwhile. (Note that fearless Achilles did not possess this virtue; he desecrated Hector's body. In victory, he was not a "good sport.")

So, let us now praise Yadier Molina of the St. Louis Cardinals. I am a Cubs fan, and the Cardinals are the Cubs' long-resented rivals, our hated Trojans, our archenemies. Yet the better to explain how baseball teaches courage during every at bat, I feel I must sing Molina's praises.

On August 8, 2016, the Cardinals are out of contention, more than a dozen games behind the Cubs in the National League Central. The Cards are playing the worst team in the Division, the Cincinnati Reds. The game doesn't matter, except to those playing and watching. It's tied in extra innings when the Cardinals load the bases. Molina steps into the batter's box. The second pitch, a 93 mph fastball, he watches swerve toward his torso—where it hits him. What does Molina do? He does not cringe. He does not flinch. He grits his teeth and grins, not even wincing as the ball makes brutal, bone-bruising contact with his ribs. Molina immediately raises his arms in a triumphant "V." He cries out, not in pain, but in jubilation. Molina's happy game-winning walk-off hit-by-pitch proves that pleasure and pain are relative, relative to bravery's reward in victory. I don't even hate to say it: Ave Yadier! All Hail Molina!

DON'T BE AFRAID OF STRIKING OUT

"Never let the fear of striking out keep you from playing the game." These wise words are commonly attributed to Babe Ruth. Greater than the fear of the ball hitting you is the fear of you not hitting the ball. It requires courage to face this fear of failure, which is not only the fear of losing but also the fear of blame and shame.

The pitcher standing on the mound is often presented as an iconic image of rugged individualism. The pitcher is the sheriff at the end of Main Street in an old-fashioned gun duel, with the batters lined up to face him. But it is the batter who is actually most alone. The pitcher has the catcher to confer with. They share secret signals and conspire against the hitter. The players around the dirt diamond and in the grassy outfield are arrayed against the batter, peering at him, dead-eyed, scratching themselves, blowing bubble-gum bubbles, silently wishing him ill. The batter is outnumbered, nine to one. Even the purportedly impartial umpire lurks behind the batter's box, there counting aloud all the strikes against the batter, just waiting, saving his best ham-actor's voice to declare: "You're out!"

The batter's box is as lonely as a gallows. Not only is the batter all alone, exposed and outnumbered, but he is also surrounded. The fans in the stands gang up on him. Marilyn Monroe, returning home from entertaining tens of thousands of troops in Korea, wondered aloud to her husband, Joe DiMaggio, "You never heard such cheering."

Joe responded, "Yes I have."[4]

What Marilyn and other entertainers don't know is what it's like to have tens of thousands of people booing, jeering, heckling, taunting, wholeheartedly, full-throatedly cursing you. Bats and balls may break your bones. And, well, names can also be very hurtful. What is more frightening: possible physical harm or what others might say about you? I recall a survey of American fears reporting that our most widely shared phobia is the fear of public speaking. We fear performing in front of others more than we fear heights, bugs, snakes, drowning, blood, needles, confined spaces, flying, strangers, zombies, darkness, clowns, or ghosts. Like a public speaker, a ballplayer needs courage to overcome performance anxiety. Indeed anxiety is a hallmark of modern life, a condition that social media has only exacerbated.

Even a sympathetic, friendly home crowd can pile on when a favorite seems to slump. I remember a game when #20 Corey Patterson, a highly touted rookie, came to the plate with the Cubs down and two outs but a man in scoring position. A hit would tie the game. Rookies give us hope. There is hope implicit in an as-yet blank box score. Hoping for a rally, the fans began to chant, "Cor-ey! Cor-ey!" Even after he watched strike one: "Cor-ey!" And strike two: "Cor-ey!" But after he swung futilely over strike three, the crowd went silent, everyone sat and looked away in shame, except for one frustrated furious voice carrying from the upper deck: "Number twenty, you SUCK!"

Cubs manager Joe Maddon advised his players: "Try not to suck."[5] Try not to, but if you do, there will certainly be somebody in the stands to tell you and the whole world that you do indeed suck. You will be publicly shamed and humiliated.

Fans play the part of the chorus in an ancient drama. As each game stages a spectacle of competition and action, of virtue testing itself against antagonists and fortune, the chorus of the crowd sits in judgment. Sometimes thousands stand as one in sudden storms of applause. Other times stray hecklers toss insults along with peanut shells from the bleachers. Either way, the crowd pronounces the common opinion, voicing praise or blame, cheering or booing.

Seeking praise and shunning blame tests hitters' nerves. Red Sox great Ted Williams explained that hitting a baseball is the most difficult task in sports, not only because a swinging cylinder is trying to make even contact with a rapidly moving sphere, but also because regular failure is the certain outcome of such difficulty. Hitting requires a resilient spirit. It is emotionally trying to keep returning to the batter's box. Hitting a baseball, Williams said, "carries with it the continuing frustration of knowing that even if you are a .300 hitter—which is a rare item these days—you are going to fail at your job seven out of ten times."[6]

Cubs slugger Kris Bryant echoed him, "When we start slumping, we start to doubt ourselves, which is human nature."[7]

The nature of the game and our human natures combine to create frustration and self-doubt. Hitting requires emotional courage because it is as much a part of human nature to doubt ourselves and shun public shame, to be anxious, as it is to flinch from a lethal projectile flying our way. Aristotle, who was not only a philosopher but also the first biologist, observed that humans are political, social animals. Our reactions, emotions, moods, and ultimate happiness all depend in part on the opinions of others, our friends and fellow players as well as the chorus of our peers.

Perhaps we yell, "Don't be afraid of the ball!" in order to distract hitters from doubt. Focusing on the fear of the ball hitting you diverts attention away from the anxiety of not hitting it.

THE "RAGE" IN "COURAGE"

We must be brave. We need the nerve to stand in the batter's box, to risk the bruises and boos. Okay, but how? How do we muster the courage to act? How should I teach Cecilia to be courageous?

For some, the spirit of courage is roused by competition, defiance, antagonism, even anger. Homer begins the *Iliad* by asking the Muse to help him find the words to describe Achilles' anger. The first words of the entire epic, as translated by Stanley

Lombardo, are, "Rage: Sing, Goddess, Achilles' rage." (You can't spell "courage" without "rage.")

If Achilles is the hero who embodies courage, then according to Homer's telling, his story is also a cautionary tale about courage's costs. The price of Achilles' perfection as a warrior was the deformation of his character and the destruction of those around him, enemies and allies alike. The bravest fighter was also the angriest. When his commander Agamemnon slighted him, refusing to privilege his individual virtuosity as a warrior, Achilles retreated to his tent to simmer and sulk, refusing to fight. In so doing, he abandoned his fellow Greeks to long days of slaughter at the swords of Hector's Trojans. Homer describes Achilles' rage as "black and murderous, that cost the Greeks incalculable pain, pitched countless souls of heroes into Hades' dark, and left their bodies to rot as feasts for dogs and birds . . . ."[8]

Baseball's Achilles is Ted Williams. As Achilles was the perfect fighter, Williams was, from his swing to his stats, the perfect hitter. He swung with mesmerizing grace. Tall, loose-limbed Williams whirled like a dervish in the box, wielding his bat like a scepter, stroking balls with authority. His eyes were sharp, his wrists quick, and his approach, intelligent and aggressive. "The Splendid Splinter" hit for average and for power. His 1941 single-season batting average of .406 is near miraculous: unsurpassed by any player since and seemingly unassailable. His career .344 batting average, 521 home runs, and .482 on-base percentage remain the highest of all time for a Red Sox. Williams's longest home run at Fenway Park, more than 500 feet into the right field bleachers, is still memorialized today, the seat where that ball hit painted red in Williams's honor. But that single red seat amidst a sea of green may also be seen to symbolize his isolation.

Like Achilles, Williams was driven by rage. He confessed, "I was mad at the world and mad at everyone, and I'd go to the plate more determined than ever."[9] He disdained both praise and blame. Sportswriters had no right to express a qualm with his performance. He did not deign to accept the fans' applause. In person, he was often profane and loud. He was rarely polite or gentle. Williams seemed to be driven more by the very few who booed him than by the vast majority who cheered him on. His career-long refusal to tip his cap to acknowledge the authentic adoration of Boston fans reveals a fault line in his character. He nursed his grudges in order to fuel rage. Williams chose to separate himself from others—from sportswriters, fans, and even teammates—in pursuit of personal perfection as a hitter. For him, it would always be "The Kid" against the world. Alone in the batter's box, he was the best.

Like Achilles, Williams was a war hero, a decorated Marine Corps fighter pilot in both World War II and Korea. Displaying bravery, Williams volunteered for both wars, sacrificing his prime years as a ballplayer to fight for his country. Williams also was a famous fly fisherman, a solitary pursuit well-suited to someone who so excelled in hitting, the most individualistic of athletic endeavors in team sport. Angling for bonefish and trout might seem like a serene pastime for a retired warrior, but once, when a big fish got away, an enraged Williams threw his rod and reel into the river. Just so, a frustrated Achilles unsheathed his sword to slash at the River Scamander when its waves seemed to oppose him.

That Williams never brought a World Series victory to Boston isolates him further in our memory. It does not diminish his individual achievement but adds poignancy to his story. No larger context distracts from the vignette of his lonely virtuosity. Sing, Goddess, the rage of Ted Williams. He was the epitome of excellence standing at the plate. Yet, as with Achilles, we must be ambivalent about Williams. Their individual virtuosity presents a clear iconic image of courageous action. Yet they deserve blame as well as praise. Neither hero honored his foes (or his comrades or contemporaries). Both suffered ungovernable rage. As Homer shows, such heroes' stories are exemplary but also cautionary.

A KITTEN NAMED WRIGLEY

While courage is required for action, I don't want to teach Cecilia that she must always stoke her rage to be brave. There are other ways to find encouragement. Witness the early career of third baseman Kris Bryant with the Cubs. Study the offensive statistics for his first two seasons and names such as DiMaggio and Gehrig come up for comparison. In 2015 he won Rookie of the Year. The next season he won the National League's Most Valuable Player. Yet young Bryant's excellence remains a bit difficult to see. Not only was he surrounded on the Cubs by other All-Stars and Gold Glovers, but Bryant was also self-deprecating.

On June 27, 2016, versus the Reds, Bryant had six RBIs with two doubles and three home runs. His astonishing sixteen total bases that day set a new Cubs record. Nobody had hit two doubles and three homers in the Major Leagues since 1913. After his third homer, a towering shot into the upper deck, the fans in the crowd at Great American Ball Park—in Cincinnati!—cheered for Bryant to come out and take a bow. His teammates tried to push him up the dugout steps. But Bryant refused. He would not show up the opposing team at their own home park. "I think that's the way to go," Bryant said, "be more quiet."[10]

Bryant honored his opponents. Quietly, consistently, every time he came to the plate, we expected Bryant to double or homer. You can't be clutch if you do it all the time. Bryant would perhaps present the banality of excellence if it weren't so exciting. Cubs manager Joe Maddon observed: "He enjoys the moment, but he doesn't go over the top with it. He's very old school."[11]

When we contemplate Bryant's swing, we may be reminded of Williams. Bryant, too, is tall and slender. His bat describes its arc with a smoothness that belies its power. In my mind's eye, I see his stance and setup. Legs wide, weight on the back foot. Back elbow up. He stays back. The bat rests nonchalantly upon his shoulder. Then his hips open. He follows through, letting the torque of his long legs and torso carry the bat down through the zone. Arms extended, he contacts the ball on the upswing.

That Bryant recalls Williams is no accident. His first coach was his father, Mike Bryant, who played in the minor leagues for the Red Sox and received firsthand tutelage under then-roving hitting instructor Ted Williams. Like everyone from New England, Mike Bryant had grown up idolizing Williams. He had studied Williams's classic text, *The Science of Hitting*, since he was a boy. Mike Bryant never made it big in the show himself, but he passed on to his son, young Kris, Williams's wisdom: "Hit the ball hard and hit it in the air."[12]

Yet Bryant exhibited little of Williams's rage. The Cubs third baseman seemed to be inspired by team spirit, esprit de corps, camaraderie, and cooperation. He good-naturedly took encouragement from his coaches, family, and fans. It was widely known that the wholesome young hitter had dated his girlfriend since high school and that he had adopted a little black kitten and named it Wrigley. Girls gushed over "Kris" (and, I bet, little kittens purred). Yet the kid could rake! He proved that courage can be found beyond the provocations of rage and war. As a skilled batsman, Bryant proved himself a worthy disciple of the Splendid Splinter, yet he liked to repeat another Maddon mantra, "We are good," with emphasis on the "we." Young Bryant, of course, led the Cubs to a World Series Championship, and though he has since moved on from the team (and been hampered by unfortunate injuries), I recall his postgame interview like a lesson from a reformed baseball catechism:

Q: Kris Bryant, the Chicago Cubs are World Series Champions for the first time in 108 years. How does that sound?

A: It's the best thing I've ever heard. I've never won an award as a team. I've always been able to do it individually, but this trumps everything![13]

NUMBER 42

A courageous spirit can reach beyond love of team and even beyond patriotic love of country to embrace all of humanity. Such spirit is exemplified by #42 Jackie Robinson. Robinson possessed the angry defiance of Ted Williams, but he found courage not merely in personal pride but in righteous anger at injustice. Robinson suffered and saw his family and friends suffer daily discrimination and demeaning slights in Jim Crow America. Yet he focused his anger into a cause larger than himself.

In 1947 Robinson agreed to play the lead in a scheme planned by Brooklyn Dodgers executive Branch Rickey. Robinson recalls that Rickey had identified him as the "ideal player" for this "noble experiment." As Robinson explains, "This player had to be one who could take the abuse, name-calling, rejection by fans and sportswriters and by fellow players, not only on opposing teams but on his own. He had to be able to stand up in the face of merciless persecution."[14]

Breaking the "color barrier" also required physical courage. Robinson recalls his first spring training camp: "One of the newsmen asked what I would do if one of the white pitchers threw at my head. I replied that I would duck."[15] Indeed in his first eight seasons, Robinson was consistently one of the National League leaders in getting hit by pitches.

Of course, when he got on the base paths, "fleet-footed" Robinson made the opposing team pay by proving himself the best base stealer in the National League. He also won Rookie of the Year and went on to win MVP and a batting championship, made six All-Star appearances and, in his last season, led the Dodgers to win their first World Series Championship.

In his autobiography *I Never Had It Made*, Robinson recalls the scene in Rickey's office where they debated the meaning of courage:

> "I know you're a good ballplayer," he barked.
> "What I don't know is whether you have the guts."
>
> . . . Here was a guy questioning my courage. That virtually amounted to him asking me if I was a coward . . . .
>
> Before I could react to what he had said, he leaned forward in his chair and explained. . . . "So there's more than just playing," he said. "I wish it meant only hits, runs, and errors—only the things they put in the box score. Because you know—yes, you would know, Robinson, that a baseball box score is a democratic thing. It doesn't tell how big you are, what church you attend, what color you are, or

how your father voted in the last election. It just
tells what kind of baseball player you were on that
particular day."

I interrupted. "But it's the box score that really
counts—that and that alone, isn't it?"

"It's all that *ought* to count," he replied. "But it
isn't. Maybe one of these days it *will* be all that
counts . . . . If you're a good enough man, we can
make this a start in the right direction. But let me
tell you, it's going to take an awful lot of courage."[16]

Jackie Robinson played his rookie season with the Dodgers
more than fifteen years before Dr. Martin Luther King Jr. marched
on Washington and shared his dream: "I have a dream that my
four little children will one day live in a nation where they will
not be judged by the color of their skin but by the content of
their character."[17] Jackie Robinson's example had encouraged a
younger Martin Luther King. King praised Robinson as "a pil-
grim that walked in the lonesome byways toward the high road of
Freedom. He was a sit-inner before sit-ins, a freedom rider before
freedom rides."[18] King credited Robinson's play on the field as an
inspiration and a precedent for his own fight for civil rights.

Robinson's glorious career helped bring African Americans
closer to full citizenship and bring the American dream, King's
dream, closer to becoming reality. Robinson stood alone at the
plate, made himself a target of hate, so that later all could be
judged by the content of their characters, have their virtuous
actions fairly registered in the box score. Robinson fought so that
all might play by the same rules, by the same laws, and enjoy the

same rights. His defiance served a larger social unit than his team or his race. His courage served to further the promise of America, of the democratic ideal first imagined in ancient Greece.

And he brought happiness to so many. The crowd sang in chorus, "Did you see Jackie Robinson hit that ball?" The example of his excellence, both his courage to play and his excellence as a player, enfranchised more to pursue happiness. His number—#42—is retired in every ballpark in America. His courage can encourage us all.

"We'll all wear #42"[19]

In order to act at all requires courage, both physical and emotional courage, risking pain and anxiety, whether in baseball or in other pursuits. We find courage in competition, although we may risk stoking our spirits to the point of rage. Thankfully we can also find courage in camaraderie. Homer and Aristotle saw that we are social beings, as keen to cooperate as to compete, striving to please others in order to win praise. Moreover, the courageous example of heroes can inspire and guide our actions. Be brave. Step up to the plate and take your swing.

When Dexter Fowler led off for Chicago in the 2016 World Series, he was the first African American to wear a Cubs uniform in a World Series. The last time the Cubs had played for the championship was 1945, two seasons before Robinson entered the big leagues. Leading off Game 7, Fowler hit a home run.

PRUDENCE

Q: How to think?

A: Like Alexander the Great.

I am not talking about that gorgeously coifed conqueror of all the old known world, champion of the Greeks, scourge of Persia, Philip of Macedon's son, Aristotle's most famous student. The legend of that Alexander and the Gordian Knot exemplifies creative problem solving: whosoever could untie the intricately tangled knot, it was said, would rule all of Asia, so Alexander sliced it apart with a single cut of his sword. Alexander exemplifies decisive action and resolved courage rather than how to think. It seems apropos that Alexander slept with a copy of Homer's *Iliad* under his pillow.[1]

A better example of how to think, how to apply reason, is a more recent Alexander the Great: Grover Cleveland "Ole Pete" Alexander of Nebraska, iconic curveballer. Starting out professionally in Philadelphia in 1911, Alexander immediately established his superiority, leading the league in strikeouts, complete games, and wins. He played most of his career with the Cubs, though he served the 1918 season on the battlefields and in the trenches of France with the US Army Field Artillery. He returned to pitch for

Chicago and then St. Louis. Now deaf in one ear, shell-shocked, a chronic epileptic (a side effect of German mustard gas), as well as a committed alcoholic, Alexander nevertheless proved to be the most dominant pitcher through the roaring twenties.

BRAINS, HOWEVER HUNG OVER, BEAT BRAWN

No more famous tale is told of Alexander the Great than his late-inning relief pitching for St. Louis in Game 7 of the 1926 World Series in New York. In the 7th inning, the Cards lead 2–1. There are two outs, but the bases are loaded with Yanks. The Cards' starter, a knuckleballer, has a burst blister on his first finger and can no longer even hold the ball in his throwing hand.

It's a hundred years ago, and Yankee Stadium is the only venue in baseball equipped with telephones. The phone in the Cardinals' pen rings. "Send in Alexander!" Even though he pitched a complete nine innings the afternoon before to win Game 6 and force this winner-take-all Game 7, even though (some said) he drank deeply into the previous evening in celebration, Alexander now strolls to the mound, eyeing the stocky Yankee Tony Lazzeri lurking by the batter's box. Lazzeri is part of the Yankees' "Murderers' Row," the dreaded lineup that also includes Lou Gehrig, Bob Meusel, and Babe Ruth. Each now has his plaque in the Hall of Fame. This is a Gordian Knot of a lineup, but there is no sword sharp enough, no fastball fast enough to cut right through this group of hitters.

Taking the ball from his catcher, Alexander agrees to start off the aggressive, already-antsy Lazzeri with a curve low and away, which the power hitter swings over. The catcher runs the ball back to the mound. Alexander wants to throw the fastball. But Lazzeri is a fastball hitter, objects the catcher. Alexander says that he'll put it where the only thing Lazzeri can do is foul it off. The next pitch flies right up under Lazzeri's chin; he cracks it hard and sends it high and far, ten feet into the left field bleachers, but foul. The catcher tosses Alexander another ball, squats, and signals for the curve. Alexander gives what's called for. Lazzeri swings violently through empty air. One-two-three, Alexander has struck out Lazzeri swinging, stranding three Yanks and holding the Cardinals' lead.

Back out in the 8th, Alexander induces a groundout, a foul fly, and a pop fly. In the 9th, he gets two more groundouts, then walks Ruth, who is immediately thrown out trying to steal second, and the Cardinals win the World Series! Ole Pete craftily used his full repertoire of pitches, his defense, and the Yankees' own aggressiveness to defeat them. Better than the story of the Gordian Knot, Alexander the Great's ingenuity demonstrates the classic cardinal virtue of prudence, or how to think.

BE SMART

"Prudence" is the usual translation of the Greek word *phronesis*, the virtue related to how to think. Prudence is reason in action: looking before you leap, thinking before you speak, turning your head both ways before you cross the street. But it is more than that. Prudence is carefully considering the situation in order to take the most beneficial action.

Today, however, the word "prudence" connotes caution rather than action. I can still see comedian Dana Carvey impersonating POTUS #41 George H. W. Bush, neck stiff, a high nasally voice escaping from pursed lips, like air from a balloon after the party's been canceled: "It would not be prudent at this juncture." What would not be prudent? *It*. (Note the imprecise pronoun.)

"It" is action. At this juncture, action ought not be taken. (Note the assumed passivity.) H. W. uses prudence as reason not to act. Rather than courage, here is the counsel of prudence: caution, inaction.

Of course, President Bush, not only a war hero and former head of the CIA, was a pitcher at Yale and is using the term correctly. Prudence is being situationally aware, surveying the particular juncture of the scene and the players, before deciding how to act. Prudence counsels against the recklessness of the heat of the moment. But "prudence" as just caution is the opposite of the term's ancient sense. Prudence really ought to be understood as reason in action.

In the contemporary American imagination, "prudence" also recalls prudery. The prude coldly denies sexual arousal, disdains unwanted advances along with all other forms of warm-blooded fun. I can hear the Beatles' "Dear Prudence" playing in my head. Why doesn't she come out to play? The implication is that prudence won't "play" of her own accord. But prudence mistaken for prudery is a perversion of the term. In fact, prudence is all about practicality, about using reason to direct actions more effectively. From a prudential perspective, an action is only "prudent" when it works, if it plays!

Rather than "prudence," some translators suggest that *phronesis* should be translated as "practical wisdom." But that's five syllables. By the time you get through saying to yourself, "Okay, self, now I must employ my practical wisdom," well, the moment has passed. What's happened has happened without your input or influence.

I like the word "smart." Smart implies street smarts. Smart knows what time it is. Smart knows what base it's on. Smart knows the score. My father often advised me: "Be smart." The implication was that I might be tempted to act stupidly in any one of the ways teenagers might be tempted—sex, drugs, alcohol, splashing in the town fountain at midnight in your underwear while loudly reenacting a scene from a John Wayne movie or what have you—and that I needed reminding. Really, we all often need reminding. This is why we talk to ourselves. As John Wayne was said to have said, "Life's hard; it's harder when you're stupid." Although in my Boston accent, into which I occasionally still lapse, my pronunciation of the word, even to my own ears, makes my saying "Be sm-ah-t" sound kinda dumb. Oh well. Perhaps this is a check on intellectual hubris. I've often found myself most stupid when I think I'm being clever. Maybe this is why Cecilia just nods and laughs when I say it to her: Be sm-ah-t!

ODYSSEUS VERSUS THE CYCLOPS

Odysseus is an ancient action hero whose most heroic feature is his brain. Odysseus exemplifies the virtue related to how to think: prudence, practical wisdom, smarts. Yes, you need to act in order to have any effect on the world, but in order to be effective, it is also crucial to think before you act. Acting without thinking leads to the vice of recklessness. Odysseus, the "myriad-minded," exemplifies how to think. His stories show how to put reason into action. "Sing me, oh muse, the man of twists and turns," begins the *Odyssey*.

Odysseus regales the Phaeacians with tales of his courage and cunning. The stories Odysseus tells in his own voice are the most memorable episodes of Homer's epic. Not only can Odysseus throw a discus, string and fire a bow, sail and navigate a ship, plan and command an assault, assuage quarrelsome comrades, and dream up subterfuges, he's also good at punning wordplay and taunting insults. He can look you in the eye and lie. He can keep an entire hall of reveling strangers on the edge of their benches, riveted to his every word. He fills his fantastical tall tales with sex, violence, drugs, gore, magic, madness, witches, gods, goddesses, natural disasters, supernatural disasters, a visit to the underworld, portents recalled from the past, and prophecies of the future. He's a master storyteller of mystery, thriller, horror, and action. All this, he says with a wink, is "based on true events."

In his tale, Odysseus dallies with the lovely goddess Calypso. He sails his ship between malevolent monsters of crashing rocks and a swirling whirlpool. He resists the temptation to lose himself in blissful languor in the land of the lotus-eaters. He ties himself to his ship's mast in order to harken but not succumb to the seductive songs of the Sirens. After saving his crew from the sexy witch Circe, who had turned them all into pigs, he travels down to Hades, where he encounters his too-young-dead comrade Achilles and consults the prophet Tiresias.

The most famous of the fantastic stories Odysseus tells is of his adventure on the island of the Cyclopes. Odysseus' ship lands on a remote island filled with nasty, brutish, but very tall and very strong one-eyed hominids. The Cyclopes shun cosmopolitan company, preferring to reside alone in caves with herd animals. The Cyclopes attend to the bare necessities for survival: food and shelter. They get drunk when given the chance. They are the quintessence of barbarism. Worse, they are inhospitable xenophobes. They don't feast their guests, but rather feast *upon* their guests. They are creatures of monstrous strength and so of action, but also stubbornly unsophisticated and unreflective, and easily tempted, angered, and fooled. The Cyclopes embody the opposite of all of the classic cardinal virtues.

A side effect of being smart is being curious. It is Odysseus' curiosity that leads him into the cave of a Cyclops. He wants to converse with and learn about these strange creatures. But the Cyclops traps Odysseus and his men in his cave, eats a few, and then explains that later he will eat the rest. Clever Odysseus comes up with a plan. After all, he is the creator of the wooden horse, the ploy that destroyed Troy. He offers the unsuspecting Cyclops wine—a gift from a previous gracious host—gets him drunk, and then, while the monster is sleeping, he and his men ram the sharpened end of the Cyclops' own shepherd's staff into his only eye, blinding him. Homer is careful to describe what kind of intelligence Odysseus displays, lavishing a detailed description on how Odysseus crafts the eye-poking stick with which they blind the Cyclops. It is a description worthy of the Boy Scout Handbook. It is a weapon designed by practical wisdom, craftiness, and cleverness—by prudence.

When the Cyclops roars in pain, his fellow Cyclopes come running. When they ask him what's wrong, however, the Cyclops yells, "No One has wounded me with cleverness."

Earlier when the Cyclops said to Odysseus, "Tell me your name so I can give you a gift," our hero replied, "No One." The Cyclops said, "I will eat you last, No One. Har-har-har!" A brute and a bully in a rush to laugh at his own bad joke, the Cyclops failed to detect Odysseus' ploy. He was deaf to overtones, undertones, or irony. "No one" in Greek is also a pun on the word for "cleverness" (*mêtis*).

Now when the Cyclops calls out, his fellow brutish giants hear, "No One" has wounded me, while Homer's canny listeners hear, "Cleverness has wounded me." The joke is on the Cyclops, as is the jab in the eye. Meanwhile, Homer shares an in-joke with his listeners. The other Cyclopes shrug and walk away. Unsociable by habit, they are neither curious nor caring enough to remain concerned. Odysseus and his surviving crew hide until the Cyclops leaves the cave with his flock of sheep.

They escape by grasping onto the wool and hanging below the sheep as they exit the cave. Brains beat brawn.

"WHY ONE EYE?"

"What?"

Second-grade Cecilia is asking me, "Why does the Cyclops have only one eye?" She shuts one eye and, with the other, gazes all around, unblinking.

The word *cyclops* literally means "circle-eye." Every Euclidian knows that a circle is the most symmetrical two-dimensional figure. With a single circular eye in the center of its brow, the giant Cyclops symbolizes simple rationality, the pure capacity to calculate. Odysseus noted that the Cyclops kept a well-ordered cave, with a place for everything and everything in its place. The Cyclops, moreover, kept a regular schedule, proving himself a creature of habit. Keeping to himself, the Cyclops saw to all his own needs. He was independent and self-sufficient. He could do without superfluities such as friends, family, society, tradition, art, religion, history, courtesy, or custom—all the human social institutions that serve as repositories of experience. The Cyclops does not consider Odysseus and his men as strangers for whom custom requires hospitality. Scoffing at custom as he does at the gods of Olympus, the Cyclops is actually not so stupid, he is just willfully oblivious and rude.

Aristotle said, "One ought to pay attention to . . . opinions of people who are experienced or old, or of people with practical judgment . . . for by having an eye sharpened by experience, they see rightly."[2] The rude, uncultured, unsociable Cyclopes look at the world without the "sharpened" eye of society's collective experience distilled in custom and tradition. They see with only one eye, the eye of cold, primitive reason.

PRACTICE VERSUS THEORY

None are more cyclopean in their thinking than academics. I was reminded of the circle-eyed giants when I took my colleagues from the Divinity School with Cecilia and me to Wrigley Field.

In my enthusiasm for my newly discovered ancient meaning of baseball, over the course of a season, I shared peanuts with experts in the history of religions, anthropology, psychoanalysis, philosophy, theology, mythology, and mysticism. We entertained theories about the game from every conceivable perspective. Their interpretations of the game were oftentimes ingenious, well, because many of them are geniuses.

A scholar of Jewish thought explained to me the cabalist creation of the universe in terms of the emptiness of the outfield. The grassy green open space was the Zimzum, the primal aporia or openness required for creation. (Of course, the open space of the outfield was, during the game, where there was the least action to see.)

An anthropologist dwelt upon how the fans in the stands changed their attention back and forth. He took this as somehow explicable of modern man's divided attention or lack of attention altogether. What he failed to notice was that a fan's attention ebbed and flowed with the action on the field. He talked and talked, failing to pay any attention to the game. During the 5th inning, I left him to talk to Cecilia while I got a hot dog by myself.

A legal scholar and Christian ethicist was intrigued by the third base coach giving signs in code, a symptom of the fact that someone might try to steal the signs, and whether or not this assumed a kind of mendacity inherent in the game as well as in humanity. That's right, I said, the old fat guy in the uniform fidgeting, touching his cap brim, crossing himself, rubbing his belly, his heart, and his elbows, and doing the Charleston, was not just secretly calling for a steal. He was himself a sign of mankind's crooked nature after the Fall.

A philosopher, one of France's Immortals, sat quietly eating his Chicago-style hot dog and drinking his cold beer. After five innings, he burst out: "Baseball is so boring! It gives you time to sit and think." This Gallic theorist's problem was that he wasn't thinking about the game. But then a few evenings later at a faculty cocktail party, he came up to me excited. He had figured out that the umpire at the ball game is the phenomenologist, the philosopher with the authority and understanding to "reduce the phenomenon" of the ball, observing its passage through the zone to declare it either a ball or a strike. He smiled, very pleased with himself. He would use this analogy with his freshman seminar. I nodded and restrained myself from kicking dirt on his shoes.

These are some of the varieties of not experiencing a ball game. The experts made baseball illustrate their preconceived notions. The ball game merely illustrated a theory. They weren't following the action on the field. It would be like reading Homer merely for the metaphors, without involving oneself in the action and adventure of the hero struggling to go home.

Academics tend to be cyclopian. They see with only one eye, the eye of their own expertise, the myopic eye of theory. Yogi Berra reportedly said (or was it Albert Einstein?): "In theory there is no difference between theory and practice. But in practice, there is."

There is no harm in treating the ball game as a metaphor, but at the same time, the game is really happening. Hitting is not a metaphor for courage. To hit, you truly have to be brave. Pitching is not a metaphor for prudence. To pitch, you've got to be smart.

"Prudence" in Greek was *phronesis*, which was translated into Latin as *providentia*. *Providentia* recalls providence, or the intervention of the divine in space and time, when Jove (as the Romans called Zeus) sees into and seizes onto the moment, *carpe diem*. The prudent person participates in divine providence. When what had once seemed like merely mundane life suddenly appears as the right place and the right time to do the right thing, and you do it here and now, well, then (God bless you) you're acting prudently.

PITCHING IN THE PINCH

Pitching exemplifies prudence. As such, it can directly inspire your own decisions and actions in life. To face any situation like a pitcher is to make yourself aware of the entirety of the situation and to consider what in your repertoire of skills can be brought to bear in order to effect the best outcome. If throwing a baseball exemplifies excellence, then pitching exemplifies that particular kind of excellence that involves thinking. Pitching is prudence.

The first to explain the prudence of pitching was Christy Mathewson in his biography *Pitching in a Pinch* (1912), one of the first classics of baseball literature (and a reflection on prudence worthy of Aristotle). Mathewson ushered baseball into modernity. He played seventeen seasons with the New York Giants. Handsome, well-mannered, college-educated, affable, and articulate, it was said that Mathewson civilized the ballpark for women and children. He was one of the first five players ever inducted into the Hall of Fame at Cooperstown. He remains in the top ten in career wins and ERA. His book's subtitle, *Baseball from the Inside*, might be the first use of the phrase "inside baseball," which has come to mean knowledge others don't have, secret knowledge. It evokes whispered rumors in the dugout. It is the stuff of scouts. This is baseball from inside the pitcher's head, showing how pitchers ought to think, in other words, prudently. Inside baseball steals the signs from the third base coach, puts a shift on the outfielders for certain hitters, knows the zone of this particular phenomenologist, I mean, umpire.

Mathewson tries to find the batter's "groove," the trajectory and velocity of the ball where the batter cannot effectively get his bat on it for a hit. Batters, meanwhile, try to hide their grooves. Pitch selection depends upon the batter's strengths and weaknesses. Is he a righty or a lefty? Does he like to pull a pitch? Is he a free-swinger with "a pole," or does he choke up and slap at the ball? Is he capable of turning on it? Does he have power? Should the pitcher try to get him to hit it on the ground and let the infield take it?

Mathewson explains, "One is literally to 'mix 'em up.'"[3] A versatile pitcher not only can throw the fastball. He can also throw the curve and the slider. He can change speeds. He can go inside or out. He can climb the ladder. Change the sight lines. Throw off the batter's timing. Hall of Fame pitcher #31 Greg Maddux said, "I try to throw the pitch that the hitter is least expecting."[4] Mixing up the pitches is meant to mix up the batter.

If it were just a matter of physical ability—what is a batter capable of hitting, what's his groove and what is a pitcher's repertoire, what pitches has he got to mix up—that would be enough. "To be a successful pitcher in the Big League, a man must have the head and the arm."[5] There is another game going on. This is the mind game. Mathewson notes that some catchers and pitchers, batters and managers use repartee in order to psyche out batters. Fans heckle hitters, "You suck!" (Fans heckle pitchers, "Take him out!"—three words Mathewson confesses that have "broken the hearts of pitchers ever since the game began"[6]). There's signal stealing, misinformation, a player's reputation, newspapers. Some players cannot be moved with words. Mathewson says of Grover Cleveland Alexander, "There was no getting on his nerves."[7]

This battle of minds, Mathewson calls the "psychology of pitching" (note that this is only a few years after the term "psychology" had come into common usage; Sigmund Freud was still midcareer). Mathewson explains: "A pitcher must watch all the time for any little unconscious motion before he delivers the ball."[8]

Beyond the physical and the psychological battle between pitcher and hitter, Mathewson draws attention to the overall pressure of the game, or in some cases, of a series or a season. What is the count? What has this batter seen so far in this at bat? What has the pitcher shown the opposing team so far in this game? Does this batter have speed, can he run out an infield grounder? Is he trying to bunt? Beyond this batter, what is the situation on the basepaths? Is there a threat to steal? Is there a man in scoring position? Are the bases loaded? Does the pitcher need to go for a strikeout? What's the score? Can he afford to go after this guy here and now?

You must be aware of the situation, right here, right now. This is the proverbial, providential "pinch" where and when you must choose what to do, the right pitch to throw. Mathewson warns that some players are prone to "weakening in the pinches."[9] Here we see the connection between prudence and emotional courage. The pinch is the here and the now in the game situation, but it is also within your mind.

THE DUKE OF HAVANA

Consider #26 Orlando "El Duque" Hernández, who comes in for the White Sox during the 2005 American League Division Series versus the Red Sox. The White Sox are winning 4–3 in the 6th inning. But the bases are loaded with Red Sox, and there are no outs. The White Sox are playing to go to the American League Championship Series and then on to their first World Series in over eighty years, which they've not been to since Shoeless Joe Jackson's infamous "Black Sox" threw the game for gamblers. Hernández is a veteran from Cuba. His true age is uncertain. Like Odysseus, he arrived on foreign shores on a raft with nothing but a reputation and the virtuosity to prove its worth.

In a scene recalling Alexander the Great, El Duque throws from a Chinese menu. He changes arm angle and release point. He is outside. High. Low. Sometimes the pitch peels away. Sometimes it seems to rise. The world suddenly looks like fun-house mirrors for the Red Sox hitters.

After two balls and a strike, Hernández induces a foul pop-up for an out.

To the next batter, he throws a strike, then a ball—over, then out—then again: strike and ball. Leg kick. Side arm. Hernández flirts with the zone, and the batter fouls it off. Then another ball. It's a full count. A base on balls would surrender the lead. Hernández refuses to surrender. The batter fights pitches off foul until on the tenth pitch of the at bat, he hits it fair, hits it high, and as White Sox announcer Hawk Harrelson would say, "Can of corn": Out!

Now with two outs and the Boston base runners antsy, Hernández again runs the count full. Here he earns the respect of the batter (Johnny Damon) with a breaking ball, then he gets him swinging behind the fastball, which is (truth be told) not that fast. Out!

Lame pop fair after lame pop foul, followed by lame, half-swinging strikeout.

El Duque threw twenty-one pitches in the pinch. Inning over. The White Sox will win the Division, then the Pennant. In the World Series, the White Sox will have four dominant starters who each throw complete games—José Contreras, Mark Buehrle, Jon Garland, and Freddy Garcia—and will sweep the Houston Astros. Yet victory seemed to follow from Hernández's unforgettable performance in the pinch.

Christy Mathewson observes, "It is in the pinch that the pitcher shows whether or not he is a Big Leaguer. He must have something besides curves then. He needs a head, and he has to use it."[10] Could there be a better description of the ancient virtue of prudence? Pitching involves intelligence gathering, psychological warfare, and special ops. Odysseus would've been a helluva pitcher.

TEMPERANCE

Courage is the virtue of the will. Prudence, the virtue of reason. In addition to willing and reasoning, we also desire, we want. The virtue associated with want and desire, with our appetites, is temperance. Temperance is the quality of character required to control our urges, to be calm and cool. Act bravely. Think prudently. And react temperately. At least we ought to. To train our reactions, we pursue temperance in four ways: temperance as moderation, as the mean, as sublimation, and as habituation.

Among the famous sayings carved above the gates at Delphi, home to the oracle of Apollo, was *meden agan* (μηδὲν ἄγαν): "nothing in excess." This is the lesson of moderation. "Everything in moderation." Indeed moderation is a virtue I must teach Cecilia: No, she may not have more cotton candy. Philosophy teaches that in order to maximize one's pleasure, one must practice moderation. One ought to retire to one's garden—you could even retire to Wrigley Field—eating a single hot dog (garnished with emerald pickle relish, golden mustard, and a sparkling sprinkle of celery salt), a cup of beer, and a few choice handfuls of peanuts.

THE GOLDEN MEAN

Temperance is the mean between the extremes of our various appetites. In regard to food, to be temperate is to be neither a glutton nor an ascetic. In regard to sex, to be temperate is to be neither lusty nor a cold prude. In regard to money, to be temperate is to be neither greedy nor a cheapskate. Don't be a drunk, but don't be a buzzkill, either.

The hero of the golden mean from legend and folktale is Goldilocks, who liked her porridge neither too hot nor too cold and her bed neither too soft nor too hard. She liked things "just right." The need to find the mean is especially keen in regard to desire because our desires are many. Our desires take many forms. Sometimes we want porridge. Sometimes we want a bed. Our desires can go many ways. We need to find the mean.

Finding the mean is especially important because our desires are our motivation, why we do what we courageously do and why we think about what we prudently think about. Like an actor trying to put on a play—a play titled *Happily Ever After*—we come to a point while preparing for our role when we look up from the script (much of which we've been improvising up to this point) to ask, "What's my motivation?" You hear your cue, you hit your mark, but before you strike your pose and deliver your lines, you'd like to know why you're saying what you're saying and doing what you're doing. You step up to the batter's box and take your swing. You squat behind the plate and call for the pitch. You bravely bring a baby into the world. You take her to the ball game to thoughtfully contemplate how you're going to raise her. And you ask yourself, what's my motivation?

Our motivation, why we do what we do, all virtues aside—whether recklessly, bravely, or meekly, stupidly, smartly, or obtusely, greedily, gluttonously, temperately, or apathetically—is because of our desires. As William Blake said, "I want! I want!"[1] As Walt Whitman said, "Urge and urge and urge, / Always the procreant urge of the world."[2] Lyric poets from Archilochus to Mick Jagger make their living rendering expressions of desire in memorable music. Our desires shape our reactions. What we often don't even think about, what we don't immediately intend, this is what we must temper.

But desire, like the weather, is not always harmonious. In fact, desire tends always toward flux. Desire is infinitely various. There are primal desires: to live and to perpetuate life via reproduction, in other words, survival and sex. Charles Darwin describes this in *The Origin of Species* in terms of sexual selection. Sigmund Freud, the founder of psychoanalysis, describes instinctual desire as libido, an erotic energy that can take many different forms. What we moderate, what we temper, are our primal desires.

SUBLIMATION

Our basic base desires can take many complex forms—romantic love, parental love, religious devotion, pastoral poetry, baseball fandom. Freud called this process "sublimation," from the material chemical process where transformation of an element happens so quickly from solid to gas that it seems to bypass the liquid phase altogether. Sublimation is the process by which society channels (through child and social development) each individual's simple, selfish, instinctual desires into complex cultural forms such as art, religion, or baseball—what we like to call civilization; it's the process by which base animal instincts for sex and violence are transformed into such glorious cultural institutions as a marriage ceremony held within a Gothic cathedral or a World Series game at Wrigley Field. You might call sublimation our species' social survival strategy, or you might call it what makes life worth living. Either way, sublimation is both how we have culture and how our characters are forged.[3]

The same thinking keeps boxers from sex while training for a big fight. ("I deny them my essence, my vital bodily fluids."[4]) This is the same sort of thinking that during sex might make you think about baseball. Picture Woody Allen in bed with Diane Keaton in *Play It Again, Sam* (1972):

> She: What were you thinking about while we were doing it?
>
> He: Willie Mays.
>
> She: Do you always think of baseball players when you're making love?
>
> He: It keeps me going.
>
> She: I wondered why you kept yelling, "Slide!"[5]

So animal lust becomes love, then comes marriage, then comes (as the rope-skipping children sing) the couple with a baby carriage.

AT THE LOUISVILLE SLUGGER FACTORY

Another name for what Freud described as sublimation is temperance. Beyond simply achieving a mean, temperance can also be understood as a verb, to temper something. Metal, for example, is tempered by repeated heating, beating, and quick cooling in order to fix it into shape and make it hard. The most extreme and exquisite example of this is the forging of samurai swords. Homer describes the process: "As a blacksmith plunges a glowing ax or adze / in an ice-cold bath and the metal screeches steam / and its temper hardens—that's the iron's strength."[6] Homer employs this simile to describe the moment Odysseus and his comrades plunge the sharpened wooden stake into the eye of the Cyclops in order to blind him. Our cunning hero notes the Cyclops' staff, a large log of still-green olivewood left out to dry and thus harden naturally into a usable club. Odysseus and his men chop, shave, and taper the wood, then heat it in the fire to a glowing red point, so that after they get the one-eyed giant drunk, they can thrust and twist the flame-hardened spike deep into the sleeping monster's eye socket.

The tempering of desire focuses it and, at the same time, makes it keener. Desires thus tempered are stronger because— not blowing here and there, hither and thither—they are aimed toward an end, a goal, some good.

Wooden baseball bats are "tempered" to make them harder, the better to bear the impact with the ball. A hardball struck upon a harder bat will be sent flying with combined force in the opposite direction.

A Kentucky wood-turning shop (J. F. Hillerich & Son) was the first company to devote a full-time operation to the manufacturing of baseball bats. The story goes that in 1884, Bud Hillerich, the son of the company's founder, was at a Louisville Eclipse baseball game when Pete "the Gladiator" Browning broke his bat. Bud brought Browning back to his father's shop—previously used for making chairs and beds that were "just right"—and there and then custom-made a new bat from a good piece of white ash. At the game the next day, the Gladiator's new bat struck three hits in three at bats. Huge demand for custom-made bats followed. Bud convinced his dad to add bat-making to the family's line of business. They called their new product the "Louisville Slugger."

The first bats were made of ash wood, like the spears of Greek hoplites. (The ancient poet and soldier Archilochos sang lovingly of his "ash spear."[7]) Baseball bats are traditionally made from ash trees felled in the forests of Pennsylvania and upstate New York. Ash is strong, limber, and light. The best trees for bats grow in dense clusters where, protected from the wind, they grow straight up toward the sunlight. An ash tree needs forty to fifty years to grow to the preferred trunk diameter of fourteen to sixteen inches. From each tree will be born about sixty bats.

The trees are felled, shaved, and cut into rough billets. The raw wood is dried out before it's sent to the factory. The raw chunk of wood (often now hard maple as much as ash) is lathed into rough shape with a barrel three inches in diameter and more than three feet (thirty-seven inches or so) long. The bat's grain must be straight. Wood whose grain is angled is more likely to break. It is then sanded. A bat is "finished" by being dipped with a "filler" and hung overnight to dry, and then it is "bone-rubbed." Players used to take a bone, preferably the large femur of a cow or bull, and repeatedly rub it against the bat in order to compress the grain of the wood at the surface of the barrel. (The bone was "preferably" from a cow or bull because, in the logic of magical thinking, such a bone would seek out the baseball made of bleached cowhide—so like attracts like.) At the Louisville Slugger factory, they don't use bones, but rather a machine that applies five hundred pounds of pressure around the barrel of the bat to close the gaps in the grain to make the barrel even harder. Some players still rub their bats with the side of a bone in order to maintain or increase this hardness.

Fun aside: some Louisville Slugger bats are spun through an open gas flame. This brings out the natural grain finish of the bat. Such bats are branded with the trademarked logo "Flame Tempered." Ironically, the tempering of the flame is purely for aesthetics. It does not make the bat any harder, only more beautiful.

THE FLAME-TEMPERED SOUL

Flame tempering may be beautiful for a bat, but maybe not so much for a human being. While Odysseus could always contrive a cunning plan (or a punning lie) and had no trouble mustering the courage to act, the virtue that saw him through trial after trial, that saw him finally home, was temperance. But to learn temperance, Odysseus had to go through hell. Literally.

On the island of Aeaea, the goddess enchantress Circe captured Odysseus' crew, turning them into swine. With some divine help from Hermes and Athena, Odysseus eluded the witch's enchantments and came to a compromise with her. She agreed to transform his crew back into men. He agreed to be her lover.

After a year, although reluctant to let him leave, Circe tells her hero that, because Poseidon was foiling his return home for blinding his son the Cyclops, Odysseus had to consult the great prophet Tiresias. The blind prophet could foresee the future. Having been once transformed into a woman, Tiresias understood the desires of both men and women. Tiresias could instruct Odysseus in how to appease the gods and make his way home. The only trouble: Tiresias is dead. Circe gives her heroic lover a crash course in necromancy. She tells him what to chant and how to slit the throat of an innocent animal and pour the blood in a circle, how to fend off the ghosts that will inevitably crowd around, and how to speak to the spirit of the prophet.

When Odysseus meets Tiresias in Hades, the prophet is familiar with the hero's predicament, what has happened, Poseidon's grudge, what further ordeals he must face—and provides details for how Odysseus may overcome them. But the one bit of general advice the prophet gives Odysseus concerns temperance. He warns: "Control your urges."

When Odysseus finally makes it home, it's because he'd learned self-control from the trials he faced throughout his journey. He said no to the temptation of narcotic poppies. He had himself tied to his ship's mast so he could harken but not succumb to the seductive songs of the Sirens. He, of all his shipmates, was the only one not to eat the cattle of the sun god. The Cyclops tested Odysseus' temperance, and our hero failed that test. Unable to resist taunting his foe, Odysseus boasted of his famous name and was cursed. Odysseus will be more temperate by the time he confronts the suitors. Odysseus learns temperance by taking good advice from the prophet, but also through experience. We learn through proper instruction and practice but also through experience.

KICKING DIRT

Perhaps a ballplayer's stoic cool, his temperance, can be better appreciated in contrast with some untempered expression of emotion. Nowadays a hitter happy with his homer might flip a bat. A pitcher after pitching his way out of a pinch with a strikeout might flex and shout and stomp off the mound. But such brief outbursts, though fairly common, are merely momentary lapses of cool. The fullest display of untempered emotion comes only occasionally. When there is a close call that goes against his club, a manager will burst from the dugout to argue with the umpire. These arguments never result in the call being overturned, but do often result in ejection, which is always followed by a hot, unhinged rant and tantrum.

Other managers may have more ejections, but none offers more operatic drama than the wildly gesticulating, frenzied tirades of Lou Piniella. I may be biased. I witnessed firsthand a signature tantrum by "Sweet Lou" in the spring of 2007. A Cubs player was called out on a close slide at third near where eight-year-old Cecilia and I were in the stands. It was early in Piniella's first season as manager, the game was close, the Cubs were down, and the team was on a six-game losing streak. His reputation preceded him as smart, tough, and passionate. In fiery style, he had led the Yankees, Reds, and Mariners to great success. When I saw Piniella emerge from the dugout charging like a bull toward the third base umpire, I told Cecilia, "Watch, someone is about to get a time-out."

Piniella ran up to third base, skidded to a halt, and removed his cap. The scene seemed old-fashioned, harkening back to a time of chivalry. The choreography was well-known to all involved. Lou threw his cap on the ground. The ump raised his arm, pointed to the sky, and declared for the chorus in the stands and all the gods on Olympus to hear, "You're outta here!" Officially ejected from the game, Piniella was now free to fully vent.

The raging tirade of an "exiting" baseball manager is a kind of display of emotion rarely seen in public outside of a toddler's tired and hungry meltdown—Cecilia had already grown out of such tearful episodes. Lou brought his sweaty, pink, furrowed forehead right up against the brim of the umpire's official cap. There, up close, Lou commenced screaming his complaint. It was a Yosemite Sam mash-up of inarticulate protest, but words such as "Bad!" "Wrong!" and "Terrible!" could be heard. One worried about spattering spittle and unpleasant particulate and was happy for the umpire that he wore sunglasses. Worst was Lou's boiling-red, frowning face, a grotesque pantomime of lamentation and moral outrage, and the way he violently swayed side to side but kept his face within biting distance of the unswayed umpire. This was an atavistic regression to the prehistoric condition of the primal horde.

Other sports offer fouls and free throws, the penalty box, points deducted, flags thrown, and yards taken away, but in baseball, there is nothing in the official rules of the game that allows for human foible. This is a problem in a game where there is more failure than success. Even the best batter, Ted Williams sighed, fails seven out of ten times, but any player arguing balls and strikes is tossed from the game. On the field, any bobbled ball that costs a base is publicly marked—in all of the scorecards of fans in the stands, on a big display board that can often be seen even outside the park, broadcasted via television and social media and radio waves, and recorded for all time by sabermetricians on the internet (a data storage service originally designed to survive nuclear war)—as an error. "E" for "ERROR" on your proverbial permanent record. At the plate, you face continual failure. In the field, you are judged against perfection. Thus the stoical demeanor, the temperance that ballplayers traditionally adopt, is tested every day, spring, summer, fall. The only respite comes in cold winter. Though their cool demeanor is expected, frustration must build. Act like you've been there before. Never show up the other team. Never, never show up the umpire. *There's no crying in baseball.* The manager's tirade is the one moment when pent-up feelings, when overweening passions get their full public airing.

Everyone knew it was theater. But just as when King Lear on stage screams at a storm made of flickering lights and off-stage percussion, still real emotions are expressed and evoked. The umpire, although a man of a different generation than Piniella, knew the script and played his part well. The perfect foil, he never lost his cool. Piniella went off like a Roman candle, screaming, flashing red in the face. The ump stood by his call, hands on hips, speaking in a clear voice, shaking his head "no," begging to disagree with the irate hatless old man fuming in the sun.

Admiring Piniella's performance from the opposing dugout was Atlanta Braves manager Bobby Cox, who would retire with the record for ejections at 162. While Cox's style was rapidly chattering rabid varmint, Piniella was all ape-shit, alpha-chimp display. (At some point, it was later alleged, Piniella actually made physical contact with the umpire. Lou denied it, but said that if he had, he had not meant to and apologized. Touching an umpire would have been crossing a line. MLB fined and suspended Piniella for four games.)

Then Lou began to kick dirt on the umpire's shoes. The umpire said, "Don't kick dirt on my shoes." Kicking dirt on somebody's shoes goes back to a time when the shine of a man's shoes expressed his self-respect and his personal dignity, like the shine of his washed and polished automobile or the high-gloss shine of his armor before a joust. Kicking dirt on his shoes is to say, "Look, you have filth on your footwear, you are now unclean, profane." It is a kind of ritual act.

To the umpire's credit, he stood his ground and politely protested, "Don't do that! Don't kick dirt on my shoes!"

But Lou yelled, "I will. I'll kick dirt on your shoes!" And he did.

The ump, signaling offense, said, "You kicked dirt on my shoes!"

Then Lou stomped past the umpire to his cap a few yards away and punted it for good measure.

Later in the locker room, when asked what kicking dirt means, Piniella responded philosophically, saying that it can mean whatever you want it to mean. The meaning of kicking dirt is what a well-tempered ball player cannot express for himself, his frustration against a bad call, a bad bounce, a bad bout of luck in a long season. The manager expresses his team's fighting spirit. So when Piniella exited the field, all of Wrigley stood and cheered. "Yeah, you tell him, Lou! Give him hell!" The Cubs won their next game, breaking their losing streak. Sweet Lou lost his temper so that his players might find theirs.[8]

BREAK IN THAT MITT

There are different ways of controlling your urges and instilling temperance. Your soul can be flame tempered like a baseball bat. Put the fear of God into you. Scare the hell out of you. For the rest of your damned life, you'll flinch at the thought. This is the rote way. How to obey? Do what you are told! No, better: do what you don't even remember ever being told.

Interestingly, scholars now believe that the explicit torture scenes in Homer's epics (e.g., of Sisyphus and Tantalus) were later additions to frighten folk into being virtuous (you don't want to go to *that* hell). But in the *Odyssey* and the *Iliad*, Hades is most often depicted as a world of darkness that pales in comparison to the lived life. The Homeric vision is an affirmation of life. This is why, in order to interact with those in Hades, Odysseus must offer blood. The ghosts crave the spirit of life. This spirit of life is the agonistic and erotic energies that Freud, Darwin, and Aristotle theorized about. It is the lyric spirit that inspired the poets to pick up their proverbial (and literal) lyres and sing.

It was for the sake of temperance that the concept of hell was created and propagated, purportedly for the benefit of little children. Be good or go to hell! I don't remember ever being told about hell for the first time. I just can never remember a time when I didn't fear it. When I was a child, I thought there was a distinct possibility that I might go to hell. There were so many ways to fall into sin. If a sin was left unconfessed and thus unforgiven, well, you might be damned. Eat meat on Friday? Prepare to meet the devil! It didn't matter that I had forgotten it was Friday, that I was at the ball game and the vendor was yelling out, "Hot dogs!" and oh, how I loved Fenway Franks. Tell it to Beelzebub!

Rather than flame tempering your soul with the fear of eternal punishment, which it seems to me would undermine your cultivation of courage, you can break yourself in like a baseball mitt. A new mitt needs to be rubbed with oil. It needs to hold a hardball, be tied with shoelaces, and placed under a mattress for a good night's sleep. But most of all, a mitt needs to be used. It needs to catch countless balls, even if that means just idly tossing the ball into it over and over again. Just like the practice required to temper and train a player's reactions, breaking in a mitt requires constant repetition. You need to do something over and over to temper your reactions because reason alone does not suffice. Good reasons are never good enough to do good. Otherwise the brightest of us would be the best. (And this just ain't so.)

How many bats does a player go through in the course of a season? A hundred and twenty, a dozen times ten. A good glove, on the other hand, can last five seasons. The average major league career is half that, i.e., two and a half years. Practice, practice, practice. Play catch with it. Fielding is how we practice temperance.

Few exemplify the virtue of temperance better than Yankee captains Joe DiMaggio and Derek Jeter. DiMaggio patrolled center field with almost haughty superiority. Jeter's play at shortstop seemed effortlessly errorless, exemplifying perfection at the position. Each sustained success over long careers, got clutch hit after clutch hit, and led their Bronx Bombers with cool confidence to win championship after championship. DiMaggio won nine rings, Jeter five. The Yankees suck, of course, but Joltin' Joe and the Kid from Kalamazoo both show how character, tempered through discipline and competition, is rewarded with victory.

CAN OF CORN

How can you measure a player's play, from at bat to at bat, from game to game? From season to season, excellence begets such wonderings. Excellence inspires our desire for understanding, asks us to exercise our reason. How does it work?

Players make routine plays so routinely that you forget how difficult fielding is. At any given ball game, observe a pop fly and ask yourself how confident you are that you could catch such a ball, a ball that goes straight up in the air, something that old timers call "a can of corn" because it's as easy to catch as taking it down from a shelf.

Unlike throwing or pitching or running or even hitting, catching is especially hard because it's all about reaction. Pitching is how you think. Hitting is how you act. But catching, fielding the ball, is all about reacting. Fielding is something you have to practice all the time. Very few rookies have ever won a Gold Glove.

The first thing you do when you start to play baseball is play catch. With your dad. With your buddies. Even bounce the ball off a wall and play catch with yourself. Come home from school and play catch. As spring turns to summer and the days become longer, you play catch until the ball is lost in the dusk and you risk getting hit. This is how you play catch. Why do you have to play catch? Because training your reactions is a never-ending process. Even big league infielders throw the ball around between at bats. They play catch.

How do you measure how well someone fields? It's difficult. When a fielder fails to make a play, we call it an error. How many errors on average does a major leaguer make? Not many. So then how do you measure the opposite of an error, a web gem? It's not just athleticism that makes a web gem, it's the player knowing the game, knowing where to throw, seeing the ball off the bat, being aware of the situation. For the shortstop, who is universally considered the best fielder on the team, you get most balls hit at you, so you have more opportunities for errors.

I remember when playing Little League, I was afraid I was going to fail to catch a ball. I was no Willie Mays. I might miss it. Then it would go over my head, and I'd chase after it. Then I would have to throw it in, and my throw would be weak and inaccurate, and so everyone would see that not only couldn't I catch the ball but I couldn't throw it, either. In the outfield you have a lot of time to worry. You don't have a pitch coming at you to focus your attention. I backed up, pondering all of the possible opportunities for humiliating failure, and a ball came from behind me, flying over my shoulder and bouncing on the grass a yard ahead of me. Then a kid, sweaty and breathing heavy, ran past me. He was wearing neither the uniform of my team nor the team colors of my opponent, but some other uniform. He grabbed the ball and threw it. I had backed up so far that I had entered one of the city park's other fields of play.

I tempered my anxiety and moved back in.

JUSTICE

The fourth and final classic cardinal virtue, according to tradition, is justice. Justice, of course, is evoked by the courage of Jackie Robinson. #42 broke the "color barrier" in order to make America a more just society, so that everyone might have equal opportunity to be judged not by the color of their skin but by the content of their character, or as Robinson put it himself, to be judged by the box score, by how they performed, by their actions. Robinson's courage, both on the field and off, helped make the game, America, and the world more just. Here justice means being judged according to your virtue, how brave, smart, and cool you are, how you contribute to success. But this is societal justice. What does it mean to call justice a virtue, the fourth and final classic cardinal virtue?

SOCRATES' DEFENSE

This is the question that motivates philosophy's greatest work, *Republic* by Plato.[1] It has been said that all of philosophy is mere footnotes to Plato. Plato was the student of Socrates and the teacher of Aristotle. His dialogues, written in the fifth century, during Athens' golden age, are the only opus of ancient philosophy that has come down to us complete. After the philosophical tradition passed from the age of Alexander to Rome and then Rome declined and fell, and monks were running from their burning monasteries chased by hairy barbarians, it was Plato's works that they clutched beneath their rough robes and carried with them to safety. Plato's works, translated into Arabic, informed the flowering of Islamic civilization. In Latin translation, they inspired the Renaissance, the rebirth of Western civilization. Plato's importance cannot be overstated, and his most important work is the *Republic*. The dialogue's traditional subtitle is "On Justice."

All of Plato's dialogues re-create conversations with his irresistibly charismatic teacher Socrates. Old and ugly, Socrates wandered the streets and marketplaces and banquet halls of Athens asking uncomfortable philosophical questions of poets and politicians as well as of slave boys and old witches. When the oracle at Delphi was asked to name the wisest in all of Greece, the inspired soothsayer of Apollo answered, "Socrates." When Socrates was informed of this, he impiously replied that it was impossible because he knew that he knew nothing. He proceeded to try to defy the pronouncement of Apollo by questioning his fellow citizens about important subjects, such as what is beauty, what is truth, and what is virtue. Much to his surprise, Socrates discovered that, although his fellow citizens had a high opinion of their own opinions, their claims about these most important matters were not well-founded in reason, but in faulty logic following from unsettled premises. His fellow Athenians knew nothing, only they didn't know it. Socrates at least knew that he knew nothing.

Many found Socrates' philosophical quest to be very annoying. His fellow citizens finally became so annoyed with his ceaseless questions that they put him on trial for undermining religion and corrupting the youth. In his own defense, Socrates said that his philosophical conversations were the opposite of impious. In fact, he was fulfilling the pronouncement of Apollo at Delphi, truly loving wisdom and demonstrating true piety by pointing out the ignorance and unfounded delusions of those society falsely praised as experts. The jury sentenced Socrates to either exile or death. Defiant to the last and wanting to set an example of someone who had the courage of his convictions, Socrates chose death and drank poison hemlock.

THE MYSTERY OF JUSTICE

Plato was one of Socrates' youngest students. He was one of the youths Socrates was said to have corrupted. Plato had been a champion wrestler. The earliest bust of Plato depicts him with his Olympic medal. His name literally means broad shouldered. Plato was also a writer of tragedies, the most prestigious and popular form of art in ancient Athens. But after his teacher's death, Plato dedicated himself to writing another kind of play, a play not to be performed but to be read, a re-creation of the conversations of Socrates. These were Plato's dialogues, the greatest of which is the *Republic*.

At the beginning of the *Republic*, Socrates and a few companions are on their way to the city's harbor side, where there is going to be a new religious festival, part of which is a horse race—actually a relay race where the riders carry torches. Socrates is curious. But before they can carry on, their group is stopped by a wealthy and powerful young acquaintance who wishes to enjoy Socrates' famously amusing and interesting company. The question of whether or not this is fair, whether or not it is just for the rich and powerful to detain Socrates against his will inspires Socrates to pose the question: What is justice?

Out of a chance encounter and a seemingly spontaneously prompted conversation, Socrates (in Plato's telling) succinctly formulates the mystery of the idea of justice. First of all, Socrates summarizes the virtues as passed down from Homer. He explains that there are courage, prudence, and temperance—the virtues of the will, of reason, and of desire—and justice must be the harmonious balance and properly composed order of these attributes within the individual. In other words, for a person to be "just" in this sense, in this internal, psychological, or spiritual sense, means that they not only act, think, and react virtuously but also that these attributes cooperate and coordinate with one another to accomplish the right outcome. This is what it means to possess the virtue of justice, *to be* just. And one must be just in order to act justly.

Socrates admits that justice and the virtues in general are all difficult to think about. It requires a different kind of thinking, a different application of reason than the practical reason of prudence. It requires a searching reason, an asking and answering of questions, a free-flowing conversation (as depicted in Plato's dialogues). This might be called contemplation, or how to rethink things. So Socrates asks again—considering how to act justly and how to be just: What is justice? And he says that talking about what goes on in the psyche, in the mind or the soul or whatever you want to call it where we reason and where will and desire happen, is difficult, and so rather than squinting into this opaque interiority, it would be better to look outside and imagine what it would be like if society were a macrocosm of the self, if the city were the soul writ large.

Socrates talks on and on into the night. They never get to see the relay race on horseback with flaming torches in honor of some new religion because Socrates talks so much. In the course of his conversation, what will add up to Plato's longest dialogue,

Socrates describes how the city can be broken up into three parts: the merchant class, the guardian class (of soldiers and police), and the ruling class of philosopher kings. If such a city were justly organized, then the merchants, those concerned with desire, ought to exemplify temperance. The police and soldiers, those who uphold the law and protect the city walls, those motivated by honor and who must have strong wills and be ready to act, ought to be courageous. And the leaders ought to be prudent, ought to apply their reasons to the running of the city. And so justice would be the philosopher kings leading the guardians to protect the merchants and the workers, who in turn provide for the well-being and satisfy the appetites of all. Just so—macrocosm applied to microcosm—prudent reason ought to guide desires toward temperance and will toward courage. This is the virtue of justice; a well-ordered soul is like a city that works (like a team with a heavy-hitting lineup, strong starters, a deep pen, stellar defense, and a crafty manager looking on from the dugout).

UTOPIA TO DYSTOPIA

An irony of Plato's great dialogue is that in employing the metaphor of the self as city, in describing a well-balanced, harmoniously functioning, justly composed soul wherein prudent reason encourages the will and desire is tempered, the *Republic* also describes a totalitarian state. Plato's republic is a "utopia," meaning it, in actuality, is "no place." It is a construct of contemplative conversation. But throughout history some have tried to realize Plato's republic, whether reformulated after Augustine's *City of God* or Marx's *Das Kapital*, to create the most perfect, perfectly oppressive totalitarian regime. Rather than philosopher kings, there have been inquisitors and apparatchiks telling their "noble lies," their propaganda, stoking their comrades to militant violence and seizing the means of production in order to centrally plan—usually on a Stalinist or Maoist five-year plan—to realize some dream of theoretical justice. But such could not have been the intent of Socrates or Plato, who qualified his utopian book on the city with a practical dialogue about laws. Nor was it the intent of his student Aristotle, who wrote about the importance of a mixed regime in order to create a just republic, the form of government that inspired America's founders.

Obviously Socrates thought at a disadvantage. He had to create his conceit, his metaphor, his analogy out of whole cloth, conjuring an invisible city. Socrates, to his detriment, lived in a time before the invention of baseball. It's difficult to think about virtue ethics when your popular frames of reference are limited to discus, wrestling, and the occasional chariot race. You can see why he was rushing to check out the new flaming torch relay! If only Socrates could have sat in the stands with Cecilia and me, he would have seen how hitting teaches courage, pitching prudence, and fielding temperance, and how the full game of baseball itself teaches justice.

And it would have been obvious that rather than consider how all of these virtues work together in terms of a city, it would be better to posit a game, imagine a ballpark, and contemplate a team. It would be clear that just as a team must be coordinated properly in order to cooperate well and compete—that pitching, fielding, and hitting all need to be timely and excellent—so the psyche needs to think, want, and will all together so that the individual can act justly in society.

WRITTEN AND UNWRITTEN RULES

A better way to understand justice is—you guessed it!—go to a ball game. Like a society, a city, a *polis* as Socrates might describe, a ball game has both laws—called rules—and customs—which include unwritten rules. *The Official Baseball Rules* published each year by Major League Baseball covers nine discrete topics, from Preliminaries to Playing the Game to Improper Play and so on, plus a dictionary of terms and appendices over more than one hundred and fifty pages. The rules of the game have evolved. Once upon a time, throwing a curveball was not allowed. A few years ago, wider bases and a pitch clock were introduced. Both players and managers must respect the rules, yet part of competing is to play by the letter of the law.

Many Supreme Court justices have been avid baseball fans. The first commissioner of baseball was a federal judge, Kenesaw Mountain Landis. He was brought on to bring legitimacy to a game many perceived to have grown corrupt. One of his first acts was to enforce the rules against gambling on the infamous Chicago "Black Sox," including the great Shoeless Joe Jackson. Similarly Bart Giamatti, a scholar of Renaissance literature from Yale, became commissioner and banned the great Pete Rose from the game for gambling on baseball. Rose never bet on a game in which he played or managed, but Giamatti enforced the letter of the law that no player or manager should bet on MLB games at all.

Beyond the rules of the game, their letter and spirit, are the unwritten rules, the customs and conventions surrounding the game. The most controversial unwritten rule at the moment is for players not to celebrate, not to flip their bat, after a home run. If a player does so, they may expect to be hit by a pitch at their next at bat ("justice" served). The point of the custom is that baseball is a game of failure. It takes a lot of emotional courage to give your best and risk having your best not be good enough in front of teammates and fans. For one player to show up or mock another, to taunt another in such a way—interestingly it is okay, or even considered part of the game, to actually taunt another player before and during the at bat, but after the outcome, it is not all right. Similarly the pitcher, after he gets a strikeout, will turn away from the batter, his defeated adversary, before stomping and screaming in jubilation.

Implicit is that it is not the rules of the game that allow for play but rather the unwritten rules of sportsmanship that allow play to occur at all. Unlike war, wherein (proverbially) all is fair, for a game to work, there must be customs, conventions, sportsmanship. We cooperate in order to compete. We agree to come together in order to stage a sublimated version of warfare. This is what philosopher William James might call "the moral equivalent of war."[2] Warfare, James observed, pushed humans to maximize their capacities in pursuit of victory and avoidance of defeat, slavery, and death. Ironically, the worst behavior of humans brought out human beings' best attributes, their virtues. In ancient Greek terms, *agon*, conflict, fosters *arête*, virtue. War is the crucible in which virtue may be formed. But war is terrible. Thus James pragmatically, prudently suggested that society find war's "moral equivalent," an activity that fosters the best in us without bringing out the worst in us. Virtue without the violence. A good example is sports, a better one, baseball.

THE MADNESS OF AJAX

There are the rules of the game and the unwritten rules that sustain the cooperation necessary for play at all. What undermines all play and play's most important purpose, the pursuit of virtue, is cheating. In the 1990s, many players took anabolic steroids. Among the most notable stars of the era were cheaters. Mark McGwire for the Cardinals and Sammy Sosa for the Cubs, once beloved home-run-hitting heroes, are now both infamous.

(I remember reading in the paper at the time about parents naming their newborn after the two famous sluggers. I wonder what little Mark Samuel, now all grown up, thinks about his namesakes.) Perhaps the greatest pitcher and the greatest hitter of the modern era, Roger Clemens and Barry Bonds, both used performance-enhancing drugs. The great pity is that Barry Bonds, before he took steroids, already had a career worthy of the Hall of Fame. Certainly the ambition that drove him to be great in the beginning tempted him when he got older to break the rules, written and unwritten, and betray the game. Bonds's single-season record of seventy-three homers has an asterisk next to it in the official record books, and Bonds himself is not in the Hall of Fame. His greatness only adds to the bitterness of his betrayal.

A comparable moment occurred after the death of Achilles—he was shot by an arrow in his heel (but that's another story)—when the Greeks had to decide who was going to get his god-given golden armor. A competition was held, and the final two contestants were Ajax, the strongest of all the Greeks, and Odysseus. To break the tie, it was put to a vote, and the Greeks chose Odysseus. Ajax was inconsolable. He stalked away and, in his simmering anger, decided to return at night and murder all the Greeks where they slept and take the armor that he told himself was rightfully his. But the gods, knowing his mind, made the angry hulking warrior temporarily insane. Rather than the camp of his comrades, he instead skulked into the corral for the cattle, which he massacred and dismembered. In the morning, Ajax woke up covered in blood to look in horror at the mayhem he had made. Ashamed at what, in his anger, he had attempted and humiliated by what he had done, Ajax threw himself upon his own sword. Ajax realized that his love of glory had driven him to betray his honor and his comrades. He was worse than any wild animal. The gods had shown him and the world that he had strayed outside of just and civilized company.

When Odysseus visited Hades, he sought out the ghost of Ajax to comfort him, to forgive him his momentary murderous rage, and to assure him that, when his body was found dead, all the Greeks had grieved for his passing and that he would always be remembered by his heroics, strength, and bravery. Even in death, however, Ajax felt shame. He turned away from his old friend in silence, not wishing to be seen, and walked away into eternal darkness.[3]

The historian Johan Huizinga in *Homo Ludens*, his study of the place of games in culture, explains how cheats and spoilsports undermine the foundations of civilization.[4] While we debate who to invite and who to reject from the Hall of Fame, while there have since been sign-stealing scandals and there will almost certainly be future issues around gambling, fans must worry that the culture of our game is fractured. Can the game be protected from cheating? How do I hold up the game to Cecilia (or to myself)? Can I still use baseball to teach her about "playing by the rules"? Because without rules, there is no game.

THE SHIELD OF ACHILLES

Homer's *Iliad* begins with the great warrior Achilles sulking in his tent on the beach by the boats, refusing to come out and fight because he feels his commander Agamemnon had been unjust. The result is that the Greeks without Achilles are routed and slaughtered by the Trojans led by their champion Hector. The Greeks beg Achilles to return to the fight, but he, still angry, refuses. Achilles' best friend, Patroclus, asks to borrow Achilles' armor and lead the Greeks himself. After long pleas from his beloved friend, Achilles agrees to let Patroclus wear his shining armor into battle but warns his friend not to face Hector. Patroclus' plan succeeds. Wearing Achilles' armor, he drives the Trojans back. But his plan succeeds too well. He finds himself face-to-face with Hector. Rather than remembering Achilles' warning and withdrawing, he closes with the Trojan hero. Hector kills Patroclus and is disappointed to find that his foe in shining armor is not actually the great Achilles. Hector takes Achilles' armor. Overwhelmed with grief and seeking vengeance for his friend, Achilles decides to return to war.

Achilles' mother, the goddess Thetis, flies to heaven to ask the great craftsman of the gods Hephaestus to forge her son a new kit of armor. We are just coming to the climax of the war story that is the *Iliad*. Achilles is about to fight Hector. King Kong is about to fight Godzilla. Grover Cleveland Alexander is about to pitch to Babe Ruth. And, of course, the great storyteller that he is, Homer pauses, takes a deep breath, then pulls away from the action—for some five hundred lines!—to offer a lengthy description of the craftsman in his studio, the artist in his atelier, the crippled god at his fiery furnace with hammer and anvil forging new armor for Achilles.[5]

Most of the description is of the great round shield, a shield of bronze decorated with silver, gold, and enamel. Upon the shield, the god depicts society and nature, civilization and cosmos. At the center are the sun and the moon amid identifiable constellations of the Olympian gods. Then there are two cities. A city at peace, such as the Greeks left back on their islands, where a marriage is taking place as well as civil litigation. And a city at war, such as Troy, under siege. Surrounding the two cities are scenes of viticulture and agriculture, and after picking grapes and plowing fields, young lads and lasses dance to music. Nearby, shepherds and their dogs try to fight off lions from eating their cattle. Surrounding the edge of the great shield, and so encircling this grand depiction of human political and cultural life, is the ocean.

Homer's description of the shield of Achilles is a glorious vision presented in fantastic poetry, a series of tour de force scenes presenting the Mediterranean world at war and at peace, at work and at play, cooperating (at the marriage altar) and competing (in court). The shield is mirror-like, reflecting the world it depicts.

The poet has presaged the great analogy of the philosopher. Plato described an analogy of the city as a macrocosm of the soul. In the telling of the philosopher, the city's prudent leaders justly guide its brave guardians and moderate merchants and workers. So the psyche's reason leads its will and desires. So you think before you act and react. But if all of philosophy can be said to be footnotes to Plato, then all of Plato may be better understood as commentary on Homer. What Plato explains, Homer expresses.

By showing all of civilization on the armor of the warrior, Homer implies his own grand analogy: the means of war and peace, and work and play, are embodied in the soul of the great hero. The love of Achilles for his fallen friend, the anger of Achilles at his rival Hector, are distilled into a single figure, his monumental physique encased in gleaming metal, accessorized with sword and spear and the great shield held before him. Homer's hero is the measure of all things. The heroic soul coordinates and reverberates with society and nature, the city and the cosmos.

Here we see an added aspect of Homer's poetic expression, something that Plato's philosophical explanation never gets to (and makes us see why maybe the philosopher banished the singing poet from his city). For Homer, the analogy is not simply between city and soul; the analogy is between city, soul, and cosmos, the revolving heavens above and the surrounding seas.

Homer's symbol, like his myth, does not claim to be the conceit of reason, nor is it limited to what reason can explain. The shield of Achilles is an epiphany, a mystical vision akin to the revelation of Krishna to the archer Arjuna in the *Bhagavad Gita*.

And maybe it's this cosmic aspect of the heroic Homeric vision that distinguishes the poet from the philosopher. You see, something else is at play in this depiction. Homer describes an object: a shield and the pictures upon it. But then as he describes the scenes, the people and animals seem to come to life. Someone brings someone a goblet of wine and they drink it. And the wine, somehow we know, is cool and tastes sweet. The dogs chasing the lion bark. We hear them. And as the waves that surround the world roll on, we seem to feel the spray of the surf. Somehow the art of Hephaestus—or is it the art of the poet Homer—has brought the great scene to life for us.

Whatever the source—thank the muses, praise be to Apollo!—it is magical. Homer is not laying out an analogy as part of an argument using evidence and logic in order to persuade our reason and solicit our rational consent. Homer invokes the muses and invites our imaginations so that we may lose ourselves in a reverie. His words combine music and imagery so that we are there. We see the god limping toward the furnace and drawing the glowing disc from the hot flames. Then we see the scenes there depicted and wonder, and in our wonder, forget for a moment the artifice of the shield (just as already we've forgotten the artifice of the poet's words) and see the lion jumping upon the back of the bull. We share the alarm of the shepherds and the fear of their brave dogs at the roar of the lion, and somehow all at once, we experience this symbol of strife come to life—the lion attacking the bull, the wild and civilization in conflict. Homer involves our reason, will, and desire, but he also evokes a fourth aspect of ourselves, the aspect that puts things together, makes connections, and actually creates: our imaginations. The shield of Achilles is not only celebrated as Homer's grand symbol of Greek civilization, the cause for which all the Greeks fight, but it is also the supreme masterpiece of the craftsman god, Hephaestus, and of Homer's own powers of poetry. It is an *ars poetica*, a defense and celebration of art.

The Italian mythographer Roberto Calasso mused that when Homer first conceived of the shield of Achilles in his imagination, when he first saw it in his mind's eye—like staring directly into a noon sun of inspiration—this was the moment he went blind.

The hero's shield depicts the world.[6]

SCREWBALL IN BRONZE

In 1952, W. H. Auden wrote a poem entitled "The Shield of Achilles," in which he imagines the goddess Thetis looking over the shoulder of Hephaestus as he forges her son's armor, but instead of the scenes of ancient life that Homer originally described, in the poem she instead sees scenes from disenchanted modernity. She sees people mindlessly toiling in factories and prisoners executed for ideology. It is a bleak, gray world. In fact, it is the world whose blueprint was presented by Plato in the *Republic*. It is a world from which imagination has been banished.

One thing that Thetis looks for, however, that Homer never actually in the original verse describes is the dancing, singing, feasting boys and girls playing at games. Now that Auden says it, it does seem like a lapse on the part of the ancient poet. What would have been great to see depicted would be a key moment in sport. And why not let our imaginations fly forward in time and space? The rival cities might be New York and Washington, DC, where the Giants and Senators play a decisive Game 4 of the 1933 World Series. It is the 11th inning, the game is tied, and Giants starting pitcher Carl "The Meal Ticket" Hubbell is still—still in the 11th inning!—in the game. There is only one out, and the Senators have loaded the bases. A hit will mean the game. Hubbell will be in the Hall of Fame one day. In fact, in the next season he will accomplish one of the great feats in the history of pitching: in the 1934 All-Star game, he strikes out five batters in a row, five of the greatest hitters of the time and of all time, who will all also be in the Hall of Fame, including Babe Ruth and Lou Gehrig.

That's all in the future, however. Now he is in a jam. He throws his famous "screwball." (Somehow Hephaestus depicts this on the shield.) To throw the screw, you've got to turn your arm over and twist your hand. Hubbell has thrown the screw so often that, standing at rest, his hand twists inward with his palm permanently facing out. He's a crippled craftsman of sorts, like Hephaestus, only his art is the virtuous art of prudent pitching. He throws a soft screw to induce weak contact up the middle to let his well-tempered infielders react as he trusts they will. And they do. The shortstop charges the bouncing ball, gloving it and tossing it back to the second baseman, who steps on the bag—out one!—and leaps up to avoid the sliding runner who is coming in spikes high, then slings the ball to the first baseman leaning forward, stretching as far as he can to shorten the distance of the throw, so the smacking sound of the ball hitting the back of his mitt comes a moment sooner than the runner's foot pounding the bag—out two! Game over! Giants win! The double play is an image of justice as teamwork, teammates cooperating and coordinating their thinking, acting, and reacting for a common aim: victory. Bottom of the 11th, Game 4 of the 1933 World Series would be a scene worthy of Achilles' shield. I wish Cecilia and I could have seen that game.

THE BEAUTIFUL

It's often said that baseball is "pastoral," as if in some Edenic past the game had been played without umpires amidst "amber waves of grain" with Mark Twain calling the action and Norman Rockwell painting the highlights. But the past was never perfect. And the grass is always greener in a time that no longer is (and never was). This is why it's so pleasing to imagine, why a pastoral vision is so attractive. Homer presented his version of pastoral in the *Odyssey* with the island kingdom of Phaeacia, a beautiful utopia where happy humans live and love in harmony with nature.

At the ballpark on a sunny summer day, we too can experience pastoral beauty. Modern-day gentle shepherds and nubile nymphs sit (alongside leering satyrs and cute cupids) leisurely conversing over hot dogs and cold drinks. The ballpark is a beautiful place to appreciate the game's beauty.

WHAT IS THE GRASS?

Let us contemplate the outfield grass. See the sheer gratuity of such an open landscape surrounded by the busy city. A green lawn is a hallmark of American landscape design. Other cultures like to fill their landscapes with flowers. "Grass is for cattle," they chide us. But an American likes a lawn. It is Jeffersonian and bucolic. I know. I spent summers during high school mowing lawns and weeding flowerbeds. After college, I put my liberal arts degree to good work as the gardener for Frank Lloyd Wright's Robie House, where they paid me by the hour and I watered the lawn, leaf of grass by leaf of grass. I know the romance of lawn care and why, during a rain delay, we can all take a semiprofessional interest in the groundskeeping.

Baseball is often conceived of as a country sport. Remember Robert Redford in *The Natural*, throwing the ball around the family farm near crops so tall that if he ever dropped it, he would never find it again. Sheep could be grazing in the outfield, rustic goatherds (or a young Carlton Fisk) swinging wooden staves at pitched stones.

But of course Bernard Malamud, who wrote the original novel *The Natural*, and Barry Levinson, who directed the film, were both city boys. The ballpark, like pastoral poetry, is a creation of the city made to imagine the pastoral ideal. It's always been played in the city—ask the kids playing stickball from Hell's Kitchen to Tokyo.

America's contribution to the pastoral tradition, and the world's greatest poetic meditation on grass, was written by another city boy—Walt Whitman. In *Leaves of Grass*, Whitman tells of a child who comes to him with hands full of green turf to ask, "What is the grass?" (I can testify that, soon after a child learns to speak, this is a typical question.) At first, Whitman—honest as Socrates—admits that he does not know. But then on the child's insistence, Whitman waxes poetical: "It is the handkerchief of the Lord designedly dropped with his initials in the corner somewhere."[1] Whitman holds up the grass as evidence of an ordered cosmos. For him, the grass represents our connectedness, the complex, various, pluralistic, democratic whole.

I would add a further answer to Whitman's litany, one of which he would no doubt approve: The grass is everywhere that's not the basepaths or the mound.

CHASING DOWN A FLY

Wrigley Field boasts the city's best lawn. That great green expanse, so perfectly manicured that if it were our own, we would post signs warning KEEP OFF. But the appeal of the grass at the ballpark is that it's not manicured so people can keep off it. It is kept pristine precisely to be played upon. Flying across the country, you can look down and see, adorning every city neighborhood, suburban town, and rural village, glowing emerald-green ball fields with their rough dirt diamonds. Such places, whether for professionals, college or high school players, or Little Leaguers, are a source of civic pride. These democratic vistas invite all to appreciate excellent play.

Wrigley Field has seen some great center fielders over the years: Gary Matthews Jr., Kenny Lofton, Cody Bellinger (not to mention Andruw Jones visiting with the Braves and Jim Edmonds with the Cardinals), each a dream to watch run across the grass. The grass is a perfect backdrop to the outright sprint and the diving catch. The field of green shows the lone athlete in bold outline running to meet the ball. To see the ball snatched from the air in the open field is beautiful.

But when an outfielder misses the ball, does not get it on the run or off the bounce, the aura of grace vanishes. He seems even more oafish against the beautiful backdrop of the grass. He becomes again an awkward upright ape with crooked knees and shuffling feet, no longer convinced of this evolutionary innovation: bipedalism. Wouldn't it be better just to get back on all fours

and crawl after the ball? Sometimes when the runner is round-
ing third, it seems so. Off the grass, on the dusty warning track,
the outfielder is suddenly one of us, just another guy looking for
something that's rolled out of reach. I am the same when Cecilia
has lost a crayon under the seat.

7TH INNING STRETCH

Near the bleachers entrance to Wrigley Field, on the corner of Sheffield and Waveland, a bronze statue of Harry Caray eternally leans out the window of his broadcast booth high above home plate, using his microphone like a conductor's baton. The legendary voice of the Cubs couldn't carry a tune, but he sure could strike up a crowd. Cecilia loves the 7th Inning Stretch, and I won't say I don't.

But Cecilia loves lots of things. She loves low-flying biplanes pulling banners and blimps advertising tires. She loves cotton candy (both blue and pink), hot dogs without mustard or relish, thick-cut french fries, potato chips (at this point in her life, peanuts and cracker jacks are a choking hazard). She loves the official program because, while I keep the box score, she colors over the players' faces with crayons. She loves when a Cubs pitcher strikes someone out swinging because she can imitate me punching the empty air and shouting "yeah!" And she loves when a batter hits a home run because I lift her to my shoulders to let her see over the standing crowd the player stomping on home plate, kissing the finger with which he points to the sky.

Cecilia cannot appreciate whether or not the Cubs are winning or losing. The chocolate-covered ice-cream bar in its cold silver foil tastes as cool and sweet whether it's been got for celebrating a win or for consoling a loss. As for most Cubs fans, winning isn't everything for Cecilia. It's more about how much fun it is to be a fan. For her it is simply exciting, something that appeals to her natural sense of wonder.

I face the challenge of keeping Cecilia occupied while trying to watch the game. The things that capture her attention are details that others otherwise might not notice: the couple behind us arguing good-naturedly about the game, all of the other little children being toted around, every kind of food that goes by, the advertisements, the brass band, all of the distractions that I and everyone else block out when focusing on the action in the game, she is fascinated by. What fascinates her distracts me. What is going through her mind? What does she want? She wants to touch things—the ball flying by in the sky—and make things—I dole out different colored crayons. She wants to eat more things, yes, and she wants to know things. What is the grass? She asks questions and points out various wonders of her world. (My cyclopean friends from academia looking at everything but the game itself have a natural ally in Cecilia.) She is not so interested in the players on the field when they're not moving, which is most of the time. She has not yet learned how to keep her eye on the ball. I begin asking myself how I can get her interested in the game so that both of us can watch; I end by finding myself interested in what interests her, that is, wondering at the world around us. To wonder, Plato says, is the special affection of the philosopher. This is the child's point of view, from which everything is full of potential surprise and discovery.

AH-ONE, AH-TWO, AH-THREE!

I don't remember the particular game when Cecilia first discovered the 7th Inning Stretch. I don't recall the particular month or who was playing, though I was preoccupied with particularities and practicalities, exercising my prudence, planning another excursion to the ballpark with my still only one-and-a-half-year-old child. I had brought her to many games before, so she and I were already fairly seasoned game-goers. I knew from all this experience what could go wrong and that I needed to take a lot of precautions if we were going to have a good time—if she was going to be occupied and I was going to get to watch the game.

I had four basic areas of worrisome responsibility, call them milky, dirty, nappy, and "No!" In other words, I had to make sure she was nourished, that she would not wallow for any extended period in her own excrement, that she would sleep, and (most crucial and most difficult) that she would not get bored. The prime symptom of her boredom was a rejection of the world around her, a persistent negation of all she saw and was offered to her: "No!"

I often used the first, milky, to answer the last, "No!" I used food to keep her occupied. As she got older, she could eat peanuts. We could spend hours, me opening a peanut shell, holding open the broken shell, letting her pick out a nut for herself, then eating the remaining nut myself, then letting her take the empty shell from my hand and drop it on the ground in front of us. Cotton candy was another great distraction because she could look around the stadium for the cotton candy vendor with his standard of plastic bags filled with pink and blue. We also always each ate a hot dog. We did this as soon as we got to the ballpark, because I felt that a hot dog was a choking hazard, so I watched and commented on every bite that she took, saying that some (most) were too big or that she was not chewing sufficiently. Sometimes she would tortuously tease me by taking a microscopic nibble of bun and begin to work it in her mouth with the mock-nervous mastication of an autumn chipmunk, looking at me mockingly. I didn't appreciate this bit of clever satire because if she did somehow get the perverse desire to eat the entire encased meat that way, I would be warily watching her rather than the play on the field through three innings.

A dirty diaper was completely hit or miss but usually not a problem. If a dirty diaper was our fate, I was fully equipped and knew the way to the ballpark family bathroom.

Nap was what I waited for. If she could somehow fall asleep, she would sleep through the loudest cheers. If she did not take a nap (and depending on who was pitching), my goal was to make it through the 7th Inning Stretch. After that we could be home within fifteen minutes, and I could catch the top of the 9th on TV and so know who won the game.

Between watching the game and wrangling the baby, I was largely preoccupied with practical reasoning. Seeing the world through Cecilia's eyes opened my own eyes to a different sort of reasoning—to wonder. The most perfect epiphany came seeing Cecilia see the 7th Inning Stretch. If you could witness her expression when the thirty thousand or so strangers around her suddenly took it upon themselves to stand up and sing. Apparently this is something people sometimes do. Just a moment earlier, the crowd had been a mere aggregate of couples, friends, family members, colleagues, coworkers, and lone fans communing with their scorecards. And now they were standing in unison, an army of humanity singing in harmony, "Ah-one, ah-two, ah-three!"

At first, Cecilia just observed this unexpected behavior by the species into which she had only eighteen months earlier found herself born. Without any immediately perceptible signal, but as if some genetic predisposition had been triggered, as the Monarch butterflies somehow know the way to that monastery in Mexico, the people in Wrigley Field, when the middle of the 7th inning came along, somehow "they just knew" to rise and sing.

Cecilia's big blue eyes widened. Then she smiled as if aware of something amusing, something of which those around her are not quite aware or have somehow forgotten. Cecilia loved to sing. "ABC," "Old MacDonald Had a Farm," "The Wheels on the Bus." She sang all the time, in the back of the car, in the bathtub, while she colored, or just riding in her carriage. But she sang alone, perhaps not by choice, but only rarely did an adult, much less thirty thousand adults, sing along with her. So Cecilia was soon smiling widely and singing as loud as she could. She clapped along with the crowd when the song was over and was the last to sit down. She looked to me, pleading, "Yes, again! Let's all sing it again!"

Here was an epiphany! Wonder became insight. Looking through her eyes, I appreciated and better understood what I had only before taken for granted. It was something about being a baseball fan, about being out among others, about the shining glory, the transcendent beauty of excellent individual play, but it was also about people together bearing witness, just as we sang together in sight of the beautiful green grass. Would an alien hovering over Wrigley Field in his slowly spinning flying saucer, looking down on the 7th Inning Stretch, think we were engaged in a pagan fertility ritual trying to get the grass to grow? That day I came to Wrigley with the expectation of witnessing a Cubs victory or at least of seeing a good game, competition, *agon*. What I got during the 7th inning, however, was an insight into the meaning of life. We are here to sing life's praises. "Yes, again!" This was the opposite of a hungry, sleepy child's bored "No!"

LEMME HEAR YA!

"Take Me Out to the Ball Game," in its way, is an original American hymn, a psalm, a song of praise, or a prayer. But it's wistful, touched with the proverbial "tears of things" appreciated by the old-school Greco-Roman pagans. Out with the crowd—*root, root, root for the home team, if they don't win it's a shame*—which admittedly is as likely as winning, more likely, historically speaking, in the case of those "lovable losers" the Cubs—*for it's one, two, three strikes, you're out!* Alas.

When the song was over, Cecilia spontaneously shouted, "Yes, again!" She wanted to hear it again. She was like a band-leader saying one more time, like Mozart writing out a repeat. Da capo! Take it from the top! Ah-one, ah-two, ah-three! *Take me out*... Yes, again and again. Pure praise! *Amor fati*, as the ancient philosopher said, love your fate! Love your home team. Love life! I had a feeling like déjà vu, not an uncanny feeling, but a feeling of things coming together, of things that were once far apart now being linked.

Plato in the *Republic* recommends that the young be exposed to both sports and music. Specifically, the youth of the guardian class, the class who will defend the city and from which the phi-losopher kings will come, ought to be taught sports and music. Plato develops in great detail what he means by music. He means more than simple sing-alongs, although these, of course, must be included. By music, Plato means poetry, all art and culture, in which we can include sports. Sports and music are the beginning of an education that ends with the contemplation of truth and beauty and the good beyond being.

In Homer's *Odyssey*, Odysseus praises singers: "From all who walk the earth our bards deserve esteem and awe, for the Muse herself has taught them."[1] Young Telemachus will scold his mother, Penelope, for censoring the court singer because, he says, the true singer takes his inspiration from Zeus. There is an archaic connection between art and the sacred, between music and the

Muses. Homer begins his epics with invocations to the Muses. It is the Muses, the daughters of Apollo, who reveal all true things. But note that this truth is sung. It takes the form of a song, a pleasing arrangement of sounds and words, or it takes the form of a story—even a fantastic tale about incredible heroic adventures that cannot be literally true but somehow reveals the larger truth—or sometimes it takes the form of a game.

THE SUBLIME

On August 8, 1988, Wrigley Field saw its first night game, nearly seventy-five years since the place was constructed, more than a century since Thomas Edison introduced the incandescent bulb. Yet lights at Wrigley seemed scandalous, sacrilegious, a profanation of our local *locus amoenus*, our pastoral paradise. Wrigley Field had always meant day games, baseball by the light of the sun. Surely artificial illumination would disrupt the sacred correspondences, interrupt the music of the spheres!

Ask Ernie Banks, "Mr. Cub," probably the best player or person ever to put on a Cubs uniform. Banks has the most games, at bats, and total bases of any Cubby. Other than Sammy Sosa, he's the only Cub ever to hit more than five hundred home runs. The tall, slender Banks not only gave us a vision of casual grace with his gorgeous swing—such supple, swift wrists!—but the always-smiling shortstop was also the hapless club's indefatigable voice of undying hope and unflagging good cheer. Ever sweet and self-deprecating, Banks liked to look up into the blue sky above Wrigley Field and announce, like a kid ordering an ice cream cone with two scoops, "It's a beautiful day for a ball game. Let's play two!" A double-header! "A beautiful day for a ball game," that meant playing under Apollo's shining sun. As the day was long, the game played on, but after the installation of artificial illumination, things wouldn't be the same.

HOMER IN THE GLOAMIN'

The natural beauty of the old unlit park is highlighted by the most dramatic hit ever struck by a Cub: Gabby Hartnett's legendary "Homer in the Gloamin'." September 28, 1938. The Cubs were within a half game of the league-leading Pirates. The game was tied 5–5 in the 9th inning. Darkness and haze off Lake Michigan began to shroud the field. The umpires were ready to call the game after the third out. According to the rules at the time, if the game was called, the entire nine innings would have to be replayed. Pirates pitcher Mace Brown took advantage of the deepening shadows, throwing fastball after fastball past the first two squinting and blinking Cubbies. And just so, two pitches sped by the third batter, Gabby Hartnett.

The Cubs catcher-manager had been named "Gabby" by some sarcastic coach. Hartnett was, in fact, known for his quietness, his laconic demeanor. Considered by many the best catcher of the first half of the twentieth century, the future Hall of Famer was thirty-eight years old and near the end of his career. In the top of the inning, he had thrown out Paul Waner trying to steal second. Now there were two out with no one on, and Gabby was down two strikes with no balls. It looked as dim as it did hopeless. But Gabby guessed fastball, and the ball took off into the night sky over the bleachers, disappearing into the darkness. The Cubs took the game and the lead in the standings. The fans rushed onto the field, chasing Gabby as he rounded the bases.

Gabby Hartnett would lead the Cubs to win the Pennant and face the Yankees in the World Series, which, being the Cubs, they would lose. But his "Homer in the Gloamin'" ("Gloaming," from Old English, glówan: Twilight, Dusk) remains legendary. His home run marks the distinctions between losing and winning and between night and day.

Day games were always part of Wrigley's beauty and old-fashioned charm. Most games Cecilia and I go to are day games. Day games bring more children to the park and bring out the child in all fans. Why add lights? Money, of course. Nighttime is prime time. During the day, fans are supposed to be at work. One benefit of a day game is the excuse to put aside your usual labor. If ever there was a conspiracy contrived by The Man, it was to turn on the lights at Wrigley. People protested. Around the city, you can still see T-shirts reading "Support Day Baseball, No Lights at Wrigley Field." (I sometimes wear one.) We fear that artificial lights will burn away the golden glow and sepia tones of our nostalgic park.

Yet Wrigley for a long time now has been a living anachronism, a place dedicated to preserving a way of life that never really was. Wrigley presents an ideal, the past perfected. In 1914, for example, when the park was built, Ernie Banks, an African American, couldn't have played for the Cubs. There is such a thing as progress. This is a lesson to remember while reading the classics. The ancients for all their wisdom had their faults—misogyny, slavery, near-constant warfare, poor medical benefits, limited team sports . . . I'd rather read Homer now from the comfort of the bleachers. So even as I finish my Luddite screed, I must admit I enjoy Wrigley in the evening. Baseball on summer nights is a special pleasure.

But the night of the first artificially illuminated game at Wrigley brought a storm. Whether from Valhalla or Olympus, angry sky gods threw down their thunder. A sharp lightning bolt flayed the gloom over the park. After only three and a half innings, play had to be postponed.

An evening storm at Wrigley is a stunning contrast to the usual pastoral image of baseball. The night storm provides a sublime rain delay, a rule-proving exception. Sheets of rain billow across the field. Illuminated by the great lights, the weather is caught in strobes. Then lightning flashes, and thunder shakes the old iron rafters.

> Blow, winds, and crack your cheeks! rage! blow!
>
> You cataracts and hurricanes, spout
>
> Till you have drench'd our steeples, drown'd the cocks![1]

Well, there are no King Lears at Wrigley, but plenty of fools. Entertaining drunks dancing in the downpour cheered on by happy fellow inebriates. (Dry under the grandstand and bundled by her father in sweater and rain jacket, Cecilia takes special glee in such antics.) The storm is a symbol of destructive and persecutory gods, cruel fates or capricious fortune, unpredictably violent and oblivious nature. Bigger and more powerful than we are, the storm reminds us of our vulnerability and mortality. The unpredictable weather reminds us how much our lives are subject to uncertainty. The storm signifies all that is beyond our knowledge or control.

LITERALLY, LITERARILY SUBLIME

The storm is the classic image of the sublime. This traditional use of the word ought to be contrasted with the modern usage. "Sublime" is now often employed as a synonym for the merely delightful or pleasurable—hear one supercilious snob querying rhetorically as to the delectability of his hors d'œuvres: Oh, aren't they just sublime?

Well they aren't. The etymology goes through the Latin *sublimis* meaning "high, elevated" and recalls the ancient Greek, "to look up at," as to the clouds or above to the gods. The adjective "sublime" must be reserved for thunderstorms and tidal waves, apocalyptic angels and vindictive white whales, for Zeus and Poseidon.

The ancient notion of the sublime is distilled in Longinus' treatise *On the Sublime* (*Peri Hypsous*, Περὶ ὕψους) (first century, CE). We don't know much for certain about Longinus. He remains a mysterious figure. (He ought not be confused with the Roman centurion of the same name who pierced Christ's side with the ever-after referred to "holy lance.") He was most likely Dionysius Longinus, the Alexandrian-trained Platonist and tutor to Queen Zenobia of Palmyra. Only a single fragmented manuscript survives. Yet this tattered treatise, recovered almost a millennium and a half after its composition, slowly entered the consciousness of the European Enlightenment and was translated into French and then English, influencing Addison, Shaftesbury, Gibbon, Johnson, and Burke. It inspired the Romantics in art and literature, who took Longinus' precepts for granted and conjured up all the exalted grandeur he had called for. Modern scholars of spirituality now identify the sublime with religious phenomena: the holy, the mystical, the numinous, the so-called "limit experiences" evoking "all" or "oceanic" feelings.

Longinus' focus is literature, a certain kind of elevated writing best exemplified by the grand scenes of destruction in Homer's *Iliad* and the opening cosmic creation in Genesis. But the sublime that Longinus explains is also an expression of the grandness of nature and the reflection of that nature as it resonates in the human mind.

Nature, as Longinus preaches, "has brought us into life, into the whole universe, as though inviting us . . . to be spectators at her games and the keenest competitors; . . . and if we look at life from all sides, observing how in everything that concerns us the extraordinary, the great, and the beautiful play the leading part, we shall soon realize the purpose of our creation."[2] Amen.

OBSERVE THE HOME RUN

The beautiful shows the essential connection between the cosmos, society, and our individual psyches. The sublime is an aspect of this beauty. We contemplate sublime beauty in order to better understand our place in nature.

Contemplating the beautiful game, we may intuit nature as cosmos, intelligible, ordered, and good. The sublime shows us that, although it is intelligible, nature is not, as yet, wholly comprehended by us. Although nature is ordered, that order involves chance and the danger of random violence. And nature's goodness, not our due or even our reward, requires our participation to be realized. If the beauty of baseball shows us our place, the sublime shows us how small and how precarious (and thus how precious) that place is.

Sitting at the ball game with Cecilia, I realize that if I just tell her a happy story about unsullied beauty, I will fail to prepare her for life. We must also contemplate the sublime. For even as it exposes our relative ignorance and powerlessness, the sublime, filling us with foreboding and awe, also reveals our connectedness to nature and so inspires us to aspire to better understanding and to greater purpose.

Outside of the Art Institute's sublime Turner seascape painting and the occasional Chicago Symphony Orchestra performance of Beethoven's Fifth—according to E. M. Forster in *Howards End*, "the most sublime noise that has ever penetrated into the ear of man"[3]—it is relatively rare to experience the sublime in the city. Civilization seeks to protect us from moments of violent nature. (What a special thrill to be outside, sheltered beneath the grandstand, during a thunderstorm!) After all, that's why civilization evolved, to protect us from what insurance companies refer to as "acts of God."

Aside from the occasional thunderstorm rain delay, baseball usually calls forth the lexicon of pastoral beauty—symmetry, harmony, balance, clarity, grace, springtime, sunshine, and serenity. Football, in contrast, is more readily suited to the sublime idiom. Football imitates war. Its violence is overt. Before my time, for nearly fifty years, the Bears played at Wrigley Field. Then, perhaps, with the bricks frost-covered and the snow blowing over the lawn and #51 Dick Butkus breaking through the line, like Ajax in the *Iliad*, chasing a fleeing ball carrier and, with all the ill-will of his devotedly stoked anger, jolting the bones of the poor runner (preferably a Green Bay Packer) against the frozen earth, then—the football wobbling free—we might more regularly have experienced that shudder of the sublime at Wrigley.

Yet there is a moment of the sublime that we wait for at every ball game: the home run. The home run is a sublime moment when the usual harmonious balance of the game is suspended. The fourth wall of the game is punctured when a player knocks the ball out of the park. The ball leaves the field of play. Although it's not actually invisible—see the happy Cubs fan in the bleachers holding it up, or if hit by the opposing team, see it disdainfully hurled back onto the field—and not actually immeasurable—see on the scoreboard how far and how fast it flew—leaving the field of play, the ball escapes, goes beyond, transcends the game's visible and measurable limits. Knocking the ball over the outfield wall signifies more than an easy trot around the bases and an instant increase in the score. Such a feat is a magnificent action-suspending moment that defines the parameters of play even as it defies those parameters. So the sublime homer distinguishes the world of play from all that's "outta here!"

Fans in the bleachers leap up to snatch the ball from the sky, or those outside the park chase after it bouncing down Waveland Avenue. The balance between players and fans is altered in the moment of the home run. And, of course, all of the runners come home, and the hitter trots 'round the bases with a kind of impunity usually reserved for sacred animals. (Hear Harry Caray calling, "Holy Cow!") The moment of the home run—when one of us puny mortals approaches the condition usually reserved for mythological beasts, gods, and middle linebackers—makes us search for the ancient word "sublime."

Cecilia's experience of the home run at Wrigley is something completely different. If I don't pick her up to show her what's happening, then she can't see the ball leave the park. She's sitting there when, suddenly and inexplicably, if she didn't happen to see the hit herself, everyone in the park stands up and screams, throws arms in the air, jumps up and down, and gives high-fives. Only slowly do they settle back down. I don't believe this moment for her can properly be considered sublime, but it is one of her favorite moments at the game.

MY BIG PAPI DREAM

"Sublimity is the echo of a noble mind."
—LONGINUS

I used to have a recurring dream about Red Sox star David Ortiz. He's at the plate. In comes the pitch. And—ka-whack! (bass drum and cymbals)—his bat strikes a thunderclap from the empty air. The ball accelerates up and away into the evening sky. A scientist wearing a white lab coat enters and pulls down a diagram illuminated by complex equations that describe the ball's trajectory. The scientist explains that David "Big Papi" (the pedantic academic uses his fingers to give air quotes) Ortiz has, with this swing of his bat, sent the ball (now ascending over the Citgo sign, over Boston Harbor toward the moon) at such a velocity and with such momentum that it defies not only the resistance of gravity but also the influence of magnetism. (In the dream, this nonsensical expert jargon seems very convincing.) The ball's trajectory, moreover, cannot adequately be described by current physics. It stumps Newton, Einstein, Feynman, and Hawking. A new law of physics, in fact, has been called into reality by Big Papi's bat. At this point, the scientist (surely a version of the narrator in *The Rocky Horror Picture Show* who instructs us how to dance the "Time Warp") closes his diagram like a shade, revealing Ortiz again at the plate, ready for the next ball to enter his strike zone so he may again create another entirely new law of nature. Ka-whack!

I wake up.

....

Watching Big Papi hit makes you feel like a kid again. He is affable, funny, jokey. His sense of humor is carried by his own laughter, a kind of Dominican version of dad jokes. His is the belly laughter of love. He has a sort of dad bod, top heavy. He seems to bend over stiffly at the back. Then he swings. It reminds you of the Babe, that swat. Watching Big Papi bat, you are also a kid again in awe of a grown-up, a seemingly greater being.

Apparently the kid in me still dreams of being like Big Papi.

My dream expresses a deep wish, but it also implies a deeper fear. This dream of the home run reveals the source of our pleasure in the sublime: it is the idea that human beings can take over all that they cannot control or understand. In regards to our general powerlessness, we are subject to fate and fortune. But not Big Papi. With his bat, like the wand of the magician, he eliminates fortune altogether and creates new laws of nature. And these laws can be perfectly understood and described by the best minds of modern science, thus flattering our capacity for understanding. The sublime reveals our relative powerlessness and our uncertainty. Papi and the pretentious scientist studying him are together the projected image of what we desire to be, omnipotent and omniscient, creating new laws of nature that we can condescendingly explain. Papi is a compensatory projection of all we fear (justly fear) we are not.

When Longinus says, "Sublimity is the echo of a noble mind," he seems to connect the aesthetic sublime to what centuries later psychoanalysis will call "sublimation." For Freud, sublimation was the process by which instinctual drives turn toward higher ends. So libidinous desire becomes aesthetic appreciation. This, in other words, is how civilization happens. Nature and that part of nature called human nature are both revealed in the sublime. Because nature exceeds our ability to know it, it can be best expressed in myths and dreams. My dream of Big Papi undermines the fantasies of omniscience and omnipotence cherished by rationalists and experts. Papi himself defies the moneyball sabermetrical orthodoxies that clutch is a myth. Papi's performances were mythic! He was the King of Clutch!

SWELLINGS

"As in the human body, so also in discourse,
swellings are bad things."
—LONGINUS

Another version (or perhaps it is a perversion) of the sublime came during the Home Run Derby at the 2000 All-Star Game when the Cubs' #21 Sammy Sosa won the trophy. In the finals, Sosa fired ball after ball into the outfield crowd. Torque from his legs and hips up through his comic-book superhero body generated incredible power. With each swing of the bat, all around the stadium, flashes from countless cameras went off. It seemed like Sosa was drawing lightning down from the sky. Sosa seemed himself a storm god, making the elements do his bidding, each mighty swing describing whole new laws of nature. Fans stood, mouths agape. Ooh. Aah. My memory of watching on television is particularly uncanny as it foreshadows my dream of David Ortiz.

We have since come to suspect that Sosa most likely achieved such power from steroids. Its meaning was as genuine as the lightning of flashbulbs. This was merely a virtual version of the sublime, a spectacle. Everyone knew this, of course, already. It was the Home Run Derby after all, not a game. It was just an exhibition. When Sosa was later caught using a corked bat, he pled that he only had it to thrill his fans during pregame batting practices (using it during a game was an "honest" mistake). Sosa deceived us in order to fulfill his desires and ours. Like any childish narcissist, Sosa merely wanted to be loved by everybody. To be so loved, he needed to be better than he was. We cheered him on to be better than he could be. Headlines ran: "Say it ain't Sosa."

THE BABE

"Sublimity carries one up to where one is close to the majestic mind of God."
—LONGINUS

An analogue to my dream of David Ortiz and an answer to the farce of Sammy Sosa is Babe Ruth's legendary "Called Shot." Game 3 of the 1932 World Series, Ruth came with the Yankees to Wrigley Field. Famously he lived like someone who never would grow up. Instead of playing with toys, he had wine and women. Ruth's prolific crowd-pleasing power transformed baseball. The home run king, Babe Ruth was America's first and, until Muhammad Ali, greatest sports celebrity. We can see his overweight physique, the body of a big baby to match his face. And his fabled "Called Shot" on October 1, 1932, during his final season, came at Wrigley Field.

In the shadow of the billboard advertising Baby Ruth candy bars, Ruth takes the first two pitches for strikes with the bat resting on his shoulder. Then stepping out of the batter's box—Wrigley fans jeering from the stands and Cubs players taunting from the dugout—the Babe points toward the outfield bleachers. He steps back in and smacks Charlie Root's next pitch exactly where he had pointed. Such control, a combination of power and skill, with full cognizance of such power and skill, seems to transcend the human, like something out of a dream.

That is why it is a legend. Controversy surrounds what happened. Some say they heard Ruth call his shot. Others disagree. Catcher Gabby Hartnett said, "If he'd pointed to the bleachers, I'd be the first to say so."[4] (But a photo from the event shows Hartnett with his back to the plate just when Ruth is pointing.) Twelve-year-old future Supreme Court Justice John Paul Stevens was at Wrigley Field that day. A scorecard from the game hung framed in his chambers. He said he could not say what happened one way or another.

"THE PURPOSE OF OUR CREATION"

The legend of Ruth's "Called Shot" points to the true meaning of the home run. The home run is a momentary revelation of the sublime in a game otherwise defined and characterized by a lighter, brighter Parnassian beauty. The home run punctuates the game, suddenly alters its score. It transforms the connoisseur of small ball and all the game's lovely little difference-making details into a gleefully screaming child again: You find yourself on your feet, arms in the air, shaking your fists in triumph, shouting, "Yes!" (How kids love a home run! Once in another room to clean up a spill, I left Cecilia in front of the television to watch the action and yell to me what was happening. "There's a pitch," she called. "He didn't hit a homer!" As if that's all that mattered.) The home run is a dream, a temptation, the material for legend. The home run defies the fates and woos fickle fortune. It is a revelation of the infinity of desire. It shows the fragile and beautiful limits of baseball by momentarily breaking them. The sublime makes us see our limits better, and also, in the contrast, better appreciate our place in this beautiful world.

In modern times now, many of us have lost our sense of sublime beauty. We see nature as, at best, an inhospitable environment and, at worst, indifferently destructive. All the world seems a storm. And theorized and generalized, we suspect a storm underlying every psychological and social phenomenon, a maelstrom raging in every teacup. Nature seems a meaningless void, hostile to human life but for a few crowded places where we huddle together for our mutual protection and common survival.

What are we supposed to do? Survive. Reproduce. As the classic Alaskan salmon-season T-shirt reads: "Spawn Till You Die." And console ourselves with irony.

This is a bleak vision. Yet there is something appealing in such a bleak vision. It speaks of a courage to face fearful truth. We want to smarten up. Our attraction to oblivion implies a desire at least not to be deceived, or as Aristotle calls it more positively, "the desire to understand."

But, as I will try to teach Cecilia, we need not settle for the meaningless void. We can experience sublime beauty. The sublime shows us our place in the largest scheme of things, and so long as it does not destroy us, sublime nature braces us, fortifies us, gives us a sense that we are a part of something larger and more powerful. With the help of the occasional home run, we can rediscover for ourselves sublime beauty, its pleasure and its meaning.

I only dreamed of David Ortiz. Sosa was on steroids. Babe Ruth's "Called Shot" is the stuff of legend. Yet these moments express our desire to be reconciled with the irreconcilable, incomprehensible, and overwhelming. Before the sublime, we stand in awe. Leonardo's *Vitruvian Man* is now "Jumpin' Jack Flash," yet still the measure of all things. If we muster the courage, we can observe it with wonder. And with work, we can begin to accommodate ourselves to a world not made for us or in our image but a world in which we've grown, learned to adapt, and at times even thrived.

TRAGEDY

"I'd be lying if I said that at that moment,
the curse didn't cross my mind."
**—2016 WORLD SERIES MVP BEN ZOBRIST,
RECALLING THE INDIANS' LATE-INNING
COMEBACK TO TIE GAME 7 AGAINST THE CUBS**

Walking on our way to Wrigley, Cecilia and I pass an outdoor café where two black-clad, chain-smoking sophisticates observe us and offer quick-witted commentary. Their words make me feel as if I had just wandered onto the stage at the theatre of Dionysius to be the object of commentary by a Euripidean Chorus: "Look at the little Cubs fan!" one gushed. The perfectly modulated tone at once bathed the small child in affection, the tone in which all infants ought always to be bathed, but there was also an ironic undertone at a frequency perceptible only to adult ears that told the responsible parent (me) that, as far as dress was concerned, an entire Cubby-blue ensemble could well stunt my daughter's future fashion sense, warping any proper grasp of the color spectrum. The other, after a long toke on a cigarette, with world weariness quipped: "It's never too early to learn that life is tragedy."

Etymologically from the Greek, "tragedy" means "goat-song,"

after the poor beast that was sacrificed to the god Dionysius during his religious festival of dramatic theater. Playwrights competed in retelling the sad stories of ancient myths and historical heroes. Aeschylus, Sophocles, and Euripides were the most famous winners. Only a few of these plays have made their way to us through history. Other playwrights took up the writing of tragedies, from Seneca to Shakespeare to Eugene O'Neill. But tragedy need not be limited to the theater. Anyone can recognize tragic moments in life.

The Greeks saw in tragedy a way of looking at life. A sense of tragedy is a sense of vulnerability, limitation, and finality. This tragic vision is what is often referred to as the "pessimism" of the pagans. It is most clearly expressed in the epics of Homer, who presents life as conflict and virtue as the pursuit of excellence within the constraint of individual mortality. Aeschylus said, "We all are taking crumbs from the table of Homer."[1] The tragic vision echoes through all of the reflections of Plato, who, before he wrote philosophical dialogues, wrote tragedies. Tragic wisdom is acquired through suffering, and the better part of wisdom is cultivating the prudent philosophical perspective necessary to thrive in a world that is not always hospitable to us.

THE UNOFFICIAL INTERFERENCE OF AN ENTHUSIASTIC FAN

Recall October 14, 2003. The most vivid scene of tragedy at Wrigley Field. A ball flies into left, where Cubs outfielder #18 Moisés Alou runs to meet it. The ball is falling foul toward the side wall but still seems playable. If caught, it will be out number two: the second out of the 8th inning of Game 6 of the National League Championship Series. The Cubs lead the Marlins three games to two. If this ball is caught, we'll be four outs from the

World Series, where we've not been since 1945, which we've not won since 1908.

In 1908, old-world empires declined and fell while America was on the rise. President Teddy Roosevelt declared the Grand Canyon a National Monument. Henry Ford announced the mass production of the Model T. Itinerant pianist Jelly Roll Morton combined ragtime, blues, minstrel tunes, hollers, and hymns to make jazz. And philosopher William James, editing *A Pluralistic Universe*, professed that individual religious experiences "point with reasonable probability to the continuity of our consciousness with a wider spiritual environment."[2]

I'd rather recall highlights from that happy year than tell what happens next in left field. What happens next brings rushing back all the tragic years since—years of terrorism, cold war, world wars, depression, and countless Cubs defeats.

See Alou leap and extend his arm. His glove opens. It closes, but closes upon nothing. The sound of one hand clapping, nothing, no ball. A fan, Steve Bartman, has reached over and knocked it from Alou's grasp. At the bottom of the wall, Alou looks up in disbelief. Then he doubles over into a kind of upright fetal position. He strikes the earth with his mitt, shakes his head, and shouts at the night sky.

It is important to note that Moisés Alou is not known for his emotional expressiveness. In fact, he is a philosophical, fine-tempered professional, a ballplayer's ballplayer from a ball-playing family. His father, Felipe, a former player and manager, is proud of his son because he's "tough."[3] To toughen his hands, Moisés confesses, he urinates on them in the shower. He needs urine-cured hands because he bats without gloves. In defiance of all baseball dogma and modern kinesiology, he hits from his own idiosyncratic stance, pigeon-toed and knock-kneed. This is how he taught himself, and not many, however orthodox their stance or methodical their approach, can hit better than Moisés Alou.

Cecilia and I have seen Alou in Chicago's Lincoln Park neighborhood dressed casually in loose-fitting Caribbean wear, a tropical-patterned silk shirt untucked with baggy trousers and closed-toe leather sandals. He is tall and lean with large, muscular forearms. His demeanor might easily be mistaken for easygoing. After all, he is on his way to pick up his children from summer camp, strolling beside his lovely wife on a beautiful day in a prosperous neighborhood in a nation expressly dedicated to the pursuit of happiness. But on closer look, there is an impatience to his movements. Even at his ease, Alou keeps his game face, observant and intense. When fans cheer "Alou," it sounds like "boo," and he smiles with the same simmering calm, an expression between a tough guy's reigned-in anger and the insouciant superiority of a natural aristocrat.

But now at the bottom of the left field wall—the ball knocked away—Alou succumbs to tantrum, beating the earth, yelling at the night sky. It is only momentary. He soon regains control. Throwing a long glare into the stands, he stalks back to his position. The umpires do not call fan interference. The game goes on. The Cubs lose.

Afterward in the clubhouse, Alou keeps reporters waiting while he eats a quiet dinner. He is gracious when he finally does come out. He does not blame the fan. He understands that every fan comes to the park expecting to catch a foul ball. But still, he says, he would have caught it.

The television announcers' call of the play is repeated throughout the night, repeated the next day, and after the next (last, lost) game, repeated all through the off-season. The two announcers' words accompany the image of Alou leaping, his glove open and the ball gone:

"And it's a Cubs fan that tried to make that catch."

"Why?!"

WHY?!

The question bears repeating because it has always borne repeating. It's not only what Cubs fans will still be asking themselves the next season and on into future generations. It's the question that's been asked and asked again, beyond baseball, trans-historically, cross-culturally. "Why?" is the quintessential question of tragedy.

"Why?" is a question asked by sinners at the scenes of their crimes, by prophets upon their visions of apocalypse, by historians in the ruins of empires. It's not only Cubs fans. Every thinking human being asks "Why?" The question arises out of our natural human situation, whether examined on the scale of individual heroes or telescoped to encompass entire civilizations. It's a good question. No special revelation, "Why?" is an ordinary, everyday utterance we ask ourselves with varied vehemence innumerable times between birth and death.

"Why?" is among the Seven Last Words spoken from the cross. *Eli, Eli, lama sabachthani?* "My God, my God, why hast thou forsaken me?"[4] Christ on the cross isn't making an inquiry into theodicy; He doesn't expect an answer to His question. He is praying, reciting Psalm 22:1. So even then and even to Him, "Why?" was a canonical question. In this context, it is not a question ever asked by anyone expecting an answer. "Why?" is an ancient question that never grows old because it never is answered. It is a rhetorical question meant to express grief—a lamentation at finding oneself a persecuted protagonist in life's tragedy.

Some (synthesists, syncretists) attempt to distill the history of world religions and philosophies into an essential set of opinions. But rather than any common answer, people the world over seem to share a common question, a question that all of their various doctrines, dogmas, myths, revelations, rituals, systems, and practices try to answer. No perennial philosophy, there is only a persistent question, "Why?," and that question remains ever open. "Why?" might be another question asked by the sphinx lurking in the wastelands outside the city.

Look to other shores of the Mediterranean, where Greeks and Romans put the same question to an entire pantheon of divinities. In Homer's *Odyssey*, eloquent Odysseus, with his ship wrecking around him, asks only, "Why?!" Why am I to die here in the oblivious sea rather than at Troy, where my death would have been glorious? Virgil's hero Aeneas, destined progenitor of Rome, with his ship caught in a similar storm, similarly laments, "Why?" Why must I drown rather than have been slain defending my city's walls alongside my heroic kinsmen? The Greek asks his question of Athena; the Roman Aeneas asks it of Venus. The canonical response, however, comes from Zeus, who in effect guffaws: "Why do these humans always blame us?" Zeus devastatingly turns the question back upon us, his mortal, lamenting supplicants.

A BABY'S CRY

How you ask the question "Why?" at the ball game is qualitatively different from how you ask "Why?" in the face of personal, historical, or existential catastrophe. I know this personally. I asked myself "Why?" in a moment of despair when Cecilia was born. My wife had suffered a placental abruption with life-threatening complications. Meanwhile, the doctor explained that because of the differences in blood type between mother and child, Cecilia had contracted severe jaundice. If the jaundice wasn't relieved, my daughter would suffer brain dam-age, and if my wife did not stop bleeding, she would die. The doctors informed me they had two times the amount of blood in my wife's body in her rare blood type on hand, ready for trans-fusion. This was supposed to reassure me.

I imagined a terrible, very possible, immediate future. The vision of our possible fate came in a contrast of colors: the marble white of my blood-drained wife and the waxy yellow of my brain-damaged child. At this terrible prospect, I looked up to the sky and asked, "Why?!" Of course, I did not literally fall to my knees and beat the earth. Instead I kept silent, alternating between patting my wife's cold white hand and holding our new baby daughter, gazing into her iodine eyes.

The emergency passed. Thank goodness. The bleeding was staunched; my wife was fine. After a few days in the sun and a few nights under therapy lights, Cecilia's complexion was free of yellow.

"Why?" is the first question, the question asked beneath a baby's cry. When in the womb, all needs were answered. A baby does not want to come out. "Why?" is an expression of our enter-ing the fearful unknown. For the child, the first cry expresses terror. But for the parent, perhaps the parent who had been anx-ious for the life of the child and its mother, that first cry is simply wonderful.

BLOOD TRICKLING FROM A HEART THAT'S BEEN STABBED

Let's go back to October 14, 2003. At the moment of our suffocated hopes, the tragic question came choking out, all old-fashioned pity and terror, weeping and gnashing of teeth, a convulsed expletive—why, oh, why?!

Dread entered, hope fled.

A traffic reporter in a helicopter hovering above Wrigley compared the fans exiting the Field to blood trickling from a heart that had been stabbed. We suffered a psychic wound when one of our own, a fellow fan, reached for the ball. After seeing the ball fly through the night sky, seeing Alou's glove open and then close upon nothing, we asked, "Why?" The following spring when the Marlins will have won the World Series and then gone on to cull the better part of their championship roster to cut budget, in another season's time when Moisés Alou will have moved to San Francisco to play for his father's Giants and Cubs super-slugger Sammy Sosa will have exited the team in acrimony, we still asked: "Why?" (We might still be asking it today if we hadn't finally won in 2016.)

Why did the unofficial interference of an enthusiastic fan crystallize in collective memory? Why was this single lost out—one among the minimum twenty-seven in any lost game—so fatal? Is dread contagious? In the very next minute, shortstop Alex Gonzalez will bobble a ball that should have been an easy double play. Then pitcher Mark Prior will walk Luis Castillo and go on to give up five of eight Marlins runs scored that inning. And the Cubs lineup, including Alou and Sosa, will fail to score more runs in the 9th, just as they had failed to score enough in all the previous innings.

And there was still always the next game, which, of course, the Cubs would lose, even with ace Kerry Wood on the mound. How many moments make up a game, a series, a season, a lost cause, a cursed fate?

This is what makes the tragedy of Steve Bartman so exemplary. He was an exemplary fan. Imagine the story he could have told. (A wave of nausea still comes over me just thinking about it.) He was at the game when he saw the ball come off the bat and, out of the corner of his eye, saw Alou coming close. The ball was coming right at him, right toward him, and he knowingly leaned back out of the way, made room, did not reach out, and Alou leaped up right in front of him. He saw the glove open, the details of its stitching. He saw the ball fall into the glove and saw Alou's intense, cat-like smile acknowledge him as the glove closed and Alou landed softly back on the ground. After showing the ball to the umpires, Alou tossed it up into the stands, where Bartman snatched it out of the air from all of the other reaching hands of happy fans, hands that patted his back in congratulations. He has that ball to this day, a relic of the year the Cubs finally went to and won the World Series. Oh, what could have been!

If asked why he did it, well, what can Bartman say? See his press release from the next day:

> I've been a Cub fan all my life and fully under-
> stand the relationship between my actions and the
> outcome of the game. I had my eyes glued on the
> approaching ball the entire time and was so caught
> up in the moment that I did not even see Moisés
> Alou, much less that he may have had a play.

> Had I thought for one second that the ball was
> playable or had I seen Alou approaching I would
> have done whatever I could to get out of the way
> and give Alou a chance to make the catch.

> To Moisés Alou, the Chicago Cubs organization,
> Ron Santo, Ernie Banks, and Cub fans everywhere
> I am so truly sorry from the bottom of this Cubs
> fan's broken heart.[5]

He saw the ball, and he reached for it. There is no reason to blame Bartman. And yet we do. Bartman conjures up something beyond reason. We need a cause, an answer to the question "Why?" Afterward fans in the left field stands of opposing ballparks dress up like Bartman—turtlenecks, spectacles, Cubs caps, and headphones—they mock and taunt us. This nightmare of self-replicating Bartmans captures our own nagging recognition that it could have been any one of us. Who among us might not also get so caught up in the moment that we fail to resist reaching out for a falling ball? Watching the game, we all vicariously throw or swing at pitches, run and reach for fly balls. So when the ball breaks the fourth wall between the fans and the field of play, there but for the grace of God go I.

BECAUSE THE GOAT STINKS

Blaming Bartman is just scapegoating. It is answering something that is beyond reason with our own irrationality or insanity. It is to provide a reason where we feel reason ought to be but yet is not. It is responding to the world's senselessness with senselessness of our own.

In the history of religions, scapegoating is a universal cultural phenomenon as old as human society. Leviticus says:

> But the goat, on which the lot fell to be the scape-
> goat, shall be presented alive before the Lord, to
> make an atonement with him, and to let him go
> for a scapegoat into the wilderness.[6]

This original biblical "scapegoat" escaped, but ever since, scapegoats have been blamed, persecuted, and outcast.

Local schoolchildren were interviewed after the final Cubs

loss. (In fact, it was the school where Alou's kids went to summer camp and which Cecilia would herself attend.) A majority blamed themselves. They admitted to jinxing the team by doing something out of the ordinary: eating, wearing, saying something unusual.[7] Of course, this is magical thinking. It is based upon the belief that mere mental activity can influence independent physical reality.

This kind of magical thinking is best exemplified by the famous curse of the billy goat. It is one of Cecilia's favorite bedtime stories: she often brings her stuffed goat with her to Wrigley. Game 4 of the World Series, October 6, 1945, the Cubs lead the Tigers two games to one and the series comes to Wrigley Field for the final four games. At the gate for the first home game is William "Billy Goat" Sianis, owner of the Billy Goat Tavern, sporting a long goatish chin beard. He comes with two $7.20 box seat tickets, one for himself and one for his goat. But the usher stops him and his pet at the gate: no animals allowed! Sianis appeals to Cubs owner P. K. Wrigley himself. Wrigley replies, "Let Billy in, but not the goat."

"Why not the goat?" Sianis asks at this injustice. "Why?" He brought the goat to bring the team good luck. (Why?!)

Wrigley answers, "Because the goat stinks."

Sianis raises his arms and pronounces his Greek curse: "The Cubs ain't gonna win no more. The Cubs will never win a World Series so long as the goat is not allowed in Wrigley Field."[8] The Cubs are defeated at home to lose the Series, and they don't go back—until 2016.

PRAYING TO THE CHICKEN MAN

Superstitious goat curses and scapegoating are only the beginning. People persecute themselves and one another in order to expiate sins or evils that were never their fault in the first place, but for which they lack explanation. They join cults, call crusades, issue fatwas, conduct inquisitions, hunt witches, hire psychics, whip themselves into a fervor (literally) rather than face the tragic truth that life is unfair, beyond our understanding or control. This is not philosophical, nor even rightly religious, but merely irrational superstition. I know this firsthand from my own medieval childhood.

As a child, in addition to Sunday Mass and before bed, I sometimes prayed with my grandmother. This was usually while watching the ball game on television. (I was, of course, still boycotting the Red Sox and baseball after the departure of Carlton Fisk.) My grandmother was housebound by illness. She divided her time between religious radio, cooking programs, and the Red Sox. We prayed for the Red Sox, in particular for Wade Boggs. I can still see the quick flair of his bat. Boggs swung the bat like Bruce Lee swung nunchucks: anything that came close, he hit it. The balls flew all over the field. My grandmother was no connoisseur of batting averages or on-base percentages. What she admired in "her Wade" was what she at one time had admired in my grandfather, her husband, from whom (after eight children) she had separated. She admired his spunk, his pluck, his hauteur. She compared Wade, as my grandfather could be compared, to James Cagney, someone who was quick, cocky, and tough. Much to my discomfort, sometimes she would even openly admire Boggs's strong jaw, broad chest, shapely thighs, high rear end, but mostly the way he swaggered up to the plate. For my grandmother, Wade Boggs was "a model of a man"—a hero.

Perhaps she allowed herself to admire Boggs's arrogance because it was tempered by his notorious superstitiousness. Boggs was one of the most superstitious players ever. Teammates called him "Chicken Man" because before every game, he ate chicken.

Before a night game, he took batting practice at precisely 5:17 and began wind sprints at 7:17. Once a timekeeper in Toronto tried to jinx Boggs by switching the park clock directly from 7:16 to 7:18. During infield practice, he took exactly one hundred and fifty ground balls. And before each at bat, Boggs drew in the dirt of the batter's box the Hebrew word "Chai" (יח), meaning "life." All-Star, Gold-Glove Boggs is in the Hall of Fame. For seven consecutive seasons, he had two hundred hits. After he left the Red Sox, Boggs won the World Series with the Yankees in 1996.

While my grandmother was no expert on the science of hitting, she was a devotee of portents and omens. Her prayers for the Red Sox and for her Wade were part of this cosmic matrix wherein good and evil were held in balance. My grandmother not only admired Boggs, more remarkably, she forgave him his sins. Most everyone else on television was sick, depraved, degenerate, unnatural, but when Boggs was caught in a sexual scandal, having an extramarital affair, my grandmother was first to defend him. It was not an affair; it was "true love" and, therefore, not a sin. Wade was only capable of true love. His original marriage must have been entered into under false pretenses or a misunderstanding, as my grandmother had apparently entered her marriage (which, by the way, however misunderstood or false was this union, resulted in my mother and, therefore, in me and now Cecilia). But Wade was not held back by poverty or failure, as were my grandparents. Wade had fortune and success and so could pursue true love. Now that I think about it, I wonder if my grandmother prayed for Wade Boggs as much as she might have unconsciously prayed *to* him, that "model of a man," her hero, her saint.

For Boggs, superstitions became a routine that perhaps helped him focus, but for my grandmother, superstition led to a systematic repression of the tragic truth that someday she would die.

For as long as I remember, my grandmother was sick (diabetes, cancer). She went to Mass to be healed. I heard lots of stories about all of the ways God could heal you. My mother, when not shuttling my grandmother back and forth from the hospital, was busy arranging her miraculous recovery. There was a priest who traveled from parish to parish who, at the end of Mass, lay on his hands, healed the sick, and made the crippled walk. If he did not cure you, then you could make the pilgrimage to Lourdes or have someone bring back a vial of its holy healing water. You could organize pious people from around the world to pray for your recovery. None of this worked for my grandmother, though. In the end, neither the angels nor the saints nor her Wade could save her.

SANTO'S VOICE

No sacrifice, however gratifying, can change the past. As yet there is no technology to take us back in time to the night of October 14, 2003, to aisle 4, row 8, seat 113, to tell Steve Bartman: "During the top of the eighth, you sit on your hands!" There's no such magic, so all we have is magical thinking.

Magically thinking, somebody purchased the accursed "Bartman ball" at auction ($113,824). It was ceremoniously exploded into tiny bits. The fragments were gathered and, at Harry Caray's restaurant, cooked into pasta marinara with meatballs and served to hungry grieving fans.

A publicity stunt, yes, but also a religious ritual acted out only half in jest: another half was in earnest, in unspoken, if not unconscious superstitious earnest, hoping for ritual expiation, all in lieu of an explanation of why we lost. While Alou may eat a long, quiet dinner after the game, Cubs fans must reenact a pagan ritual or a mock version of the Christian communion rite, attempting to eat and thus expiate their agony.

The ballplayer's well-tempered demeanor is akin to what is often meant by being "philosophical." Being philosophical does not mean studying logic in Aristotle's *Posterior Analytics*. Being philosophical refers to the philosophy of the stoics. It means having the wisdom to know what must be borne—life's tragedies—and having the fortitude—the courage and the temperance—to bear them. Stoicism was embraced by the Romans, particularly Epictetus, Marcus Aurelius, and Seneca. Stoicism has also been embraced by ballplayers. Suppressing any show of emotion or pain, the ballplayer keeps his intense game face, his vigilance broken only periodically by spit tobacco or a blown bubble. This philosophical perspective was eventually practiced by Alou after Bartman's interference. A ballplayer lives his philosophy by being mentally and emotionally tough. That's why "there's no crying in baseball!"

Baseball provides the proper perspective for recognizing that life is an open question. After the shipwrecks and crucifixions, baseball is wonderful. We escape to baseball, lose ourselves in the game. I did not always recognize the importance of baseball. After all, it's only a game. I did not realize the importance that a game—that only a game—can have. But ask Hall of Famer #10 Ron Santo.

Santo, the great Cubs third baseman and expert announcer on WGN radio, suffered from diabetes. He played through the disease as a Cub, but since then lost both of his legs. For such an athlete to lose his legs is difficult to imagine.

Santo manned the hot corner for the Cubs from 1960 to 1973. He was a very good hitter, but he was also deft around the bag, holding the line. After a Cubs win, he would jump up and click his heels. A gesture that was all the more wonderful given what a tough, competitive person he was. A tough man who intermittently clicks his heels loses his two good legs: a living sign of the cruel ironies life can play upon us.

But Ron Santo did not make a fuss. Well, he did not make a fuss about losing his legs. He used his affliction to inspire others to try to help fight the disease. Asked what kept him going, Santo said that it was going out to the ball game. He said that when he went to the park, he left all of his troubles outside as he involved himself emotionally in the game. My grandmother found a similar relief in baseball.

Santo's voice accompanied Cecilia and me on our long walks around the city. When you heard his "comments" on how the Cubs played—striking out, walking batters, making errors—you heard screams, exhalations, and exasperated breaths. You might think they were cutting off his legs during any bad point in any ball game, except for the fact that Santo loved the game, loved the team, never gave up hope, and so kept on cheering. His emotional, often painful, frustrating, disappointing involvement in the Cubs perhaps fortified him to face the very real physical challenges in his life. If only Bartman could have heard WGN radio instead of FOX on his headphones, maybe Santo could have warned him to let Alou catch the ball. (Sometimes I find myself distracted with such odd thoughts.)

HAIL THE GOAT!

Consider the goat: scapegoats, goat curses, goat songs, and goat sacrifices. Down to the hairs on his chinny-chin-chin, the goat represents superstition. The goat is the opposite of the love of wisdom. It is fear and ignorance, and it leads away from lasting happiness.

The goat represents our repressed desires. We come to see goats everywhere. Goats bear witness to our curses. We drive goats out with expiatory rituals or sacrifice them during aesthetic attempts at catharsis.

The goat has been domesticated since ancient times. Its cloven hooves allow it to trek the rocky landscapes surrounding the Mediterranean. Homer sings of how well-populated Odysseus' home island of Ithaca was with goats. The goat famously can digest everything and so eats weeds that are noxious to other animals. Shepherds let goats graze to clear pastures for their herds. This, perhaps, is where the goat got its reputation for taking away pollution, sickness, and evil. Goats are also associated with lust. The lusty satyr has a goat's bottom half, beard, and horns. Of course, Satan took on the image of the goat, hooves, horns, and beard dyed the deep red of blood. Ah, the poor goat. The goat also supplies a tangy, delicious cheese that is good on warm bread served with a white wine. Its hide is even used to make wineskins. The beneficent goat gives us all the makings of a symposium, including a fruitful topic for philosophical discussion.

It is no surprise that the goat would become synonymous with sacrifice and with scapegoating. It's no fault of the goat. It was just an animal that found itself in the wrong place at the wrong time. A predictable predicament, really, given that the goat was all the time all over the place. The goat has not only proven itself a successful survivor, but it has become ubiquitous, accompanying mankind throughout his adventures. There's always an innocent goat standing on the sidelines, ready to be blamed. In connection with the Cubs' sad history and especially the events of October 14, 2003, any answer involving a goat is bad.

....

Many nowadays talk about the G.O.A.T., the Greatest Of All Time. Isn't this, at least, a good kind of goat? Indeed, during the 2023 World Baseball Classic, when I watched the great #32 Mike Trout get struck out in the pinch by possibly the greatest, #17 Shohei Ohtani, to give Japan the trophy over the USA, I was ready to crown the Japanese ace and slugger the G.O.A.T. But unlike in other sports—in basketball and boxing, for example, where the superiority of Michael Jordan and Muhammad Ali are undisputed—in baseball, individual greatness is insufficient to ensure victory. After all, Trout and Ohtani were teammates for six seasons together on the Angels and never even made it to the postseason. Only after moving across town to a loaded Dodgers team did Shohei go to the playoffs—and win it all!

....

As a parent, I try to shelter Cecilia, to protect her from anything frightening or harmful. I'm glad that she was too young to fully experience the Bartman tragedy. After all, his sin was to reach for a ball flying by in the sky just as she had done so naturally as a baby. Still, I tell her fantastical stories of goat curses and scapegoats, assuring her all the while that there's no such thing as curses, that Bartman was innocent, so that she may know the difference between reality and imagination. Someday I will tell Cecilia the story of her great-grandmother, an exemplary tale of someone finding consolation in baseball, but also a cautionary tale of someone exacerbating her own tragic situation by succumbing to superstition. The result, in the end, was a loss of good faith and a final plummet into despair, which neither baseball nor prayer could relieve. I hope never to tell Cecilia what I don't believe myself. A good part of tragic wisdom is admitting one's ignorance rather than believing in make-believe. Baseball teaches us to put loss behind us and prepare to play another day. After all, it's only a game. And there's always another. I've already taught Cecilia the pithy prayer: "Wait 'til next year!"

Ave Capri! Hail the Goat!

COMEDY

Ancient tradition defines a comedy as a story with a happy ending.

On October 17, 2004, late in an already long game, the Red Sox were down to the Yankees. They were down three games to none in the American League Championship Series. And in this win-or-go-home Game 4, they were down by a single run. Now in the bottom of the 9th, only minutes before midnight with only three outs left of life, the Red Sox face the fateful figure of #42 Mariano Rivera.

Alert raptor eyes, cold coffee complexion, the tall Panamanian is the most dominant closer in post-season history. Rivera has allowed the fewest runs per innings pitched. In the process, he has already won four championship rings. His high-ninety-mile-an-hour cutting fastball breaks batters' wills along with their bats. Slugger Jim Thome expresses the consensus opinion: "It is the single best pitch ever in the game."[1] Rivera speaks piously of his pitch's origins. It is, he says, "a gift from God."[2] If so, it's an angry Old Testament God, or even older, it's from Baal or whomever Gilgamesh invoked to cast his heaviest curse. It is splintered ash wood around the plate and gnashing teeth back to the dugout. And Rivera remains aloof, all cool superiority, a figure of seemingly unappealable doom, of sealed fate: the closer comes out and the curtain falls. When Rivera takes the mound, fat ladies in the stands begin to clear their throats.

First up for the Sox is #15 Kevin Millar. Red Sox manager Terry Francona affectionately calls Millar "the fat guy."[3] Millar calls his own team a band of happy-go-lucky "idiots."[4] Big in his baggy uniform and with as much bluster as bravery, Millar marches to the plate, a seemingly easy sacrificial victim to Rivera's fastball. But minutes before midnight, whatever deity gave Rivera his pitch has stolen his control. And Millar, exercising exceptional patience at the plate, ducks under ball four and trots off to first.

Francona immediately pulls Millar off the base to put in a pinch runner: #31 Dave Roberts. A new face. Roberts had just been signed to the team at the end of the regular season. He is an action figure fresh out of the box on Christmas morning. With a cleanly trimmed goatee and a lean physique in his immaculate new uniform, everything about Roberts bespeaks professionalism and fast-twitch muscle tissue.

Francona does not say a word. He just winks to Roberts, who knows why he is in the game. Everybody knows. It might as well have been announced to the crowd: "Now running for fat, affable Kevin Millar, in a last-ditch bid to save the Red Sox season, Dave Roberts will attempt to get into scoring position by stealing second base." The Yankees all know. Before he offers another pitch, Rivera thrice throws over to first. But each time Roberts dives back to the bag safely, and each time he bounces back to his feet, brushes the dirt from his now-game-christened jersey, then deliberately paces out another long lead. Every fan in Fenway knows. Everyone watching at home knows.

I whisper to five-year-old Cecilia asleep in my lap: "That man is going to run."

Later Roberts recalls telling himself, "Seize the moment and make something happen."[5] *Carpe diem*, "seize the day," is the favorite maxim of the Stoic philosophers. Making something happen requires more than talking to yourself, of course. It requires natural-born foot speed and the finely honed, well-tempered skill of a sprinter, talent and skill for which the Red Sox signed Roberts. Making something happen requires perspicuity, or prudence, as we—you, Homer, Plato, and me—would say. (We know that Roberts, now the long-serving, two World Series–winning Dodgers manager, is smart.)

Calculate the time it takes a pitcher to deliver home. Add to that the time it takes the catcher to throw (127 feet, 3 inches) to second. Plus whatever half-an-instant an infielder requires to apply the tag. Now how fast the runner can move from first to second, 90 feet, minus a daringly long lead. Such factors inform any base thief's calculations before calculation must stop and the runner must bravely be off.

Roberts is off, head down, arms and legs pumping, a flat-out sprint. Running is the purest of athletic pursuits, the reason we evolved to move on two legs. See it painted on the side of any Grecian urn. See the earth wiped away at an archaeological dig to reveal a black-and-red urn (now on display in the antiquities collection of the Museum of Fine Arts in Boston on the other side of the fens from Fenway Park) bearing the image of a sprinting Dave Roberts. The fleet-footed warrior caught in the blink of an eye strikes the same dynamic pose as Roberts, who now slides as the ball arrives, and the tag applied. But he is safe!

Safe!

Everyone knew! It was a fully formed thought in the collective consciousness. Merely the best of intentions, but now transformed, via the virtuoso thievery of Dave Roberts, into reality. It happened.

MY BIG PAPI DREAM COMES TRUE

For the Red Sox and their fans, the meaning of "The Steal" has become clear. It meant victory. It meant happiness. "The Steal" moved more than a man into scoring position. It changed the course of events, it changed history for Boston. It changed the story the team and their fans will ever after tell themselves. It altered the mythic mindscape of Red Sox Nation. In the pivotal game in the pivotal series between two of sports' most antagonistic antagonists, "The Steal" turned things Boston's way.

The next batter, #32 Bill Mueller, singles, sending Roberts around third and home to score without a slide. Tie game!

When next David Ortiz walks to the plate in the 12th, and, oh Papi, blasts one into the right field bleachers—a home run! Red Sox win!—it is past midnight, a new day. Suddenly all appears preordained. Like something out of a dream.

The Sox take the next game at Fenway, then two more in the Bronx. So they take the Pennant. In the World Series, they sweep the Cardinals, winning it all in St. Louis. The Red Sox had not won the World Series in eighty-six years, not since they sold away to the rival Yankees young Herman "The Babe" Ruth for cold cash.

(Of course, for New York and their Yankees, "The Steal" began a different kind of story. "The Steal" distracted Rivera. It filled his teammates with doubt. After they lost that one game, doubt turned into dread. The Yankees choked.)

A NEW BEGINNING

The Red Sox World Series victory on the shores of the Mississippi was poetically punctuated by a lunar eclipse. I draw attention to this portent. This was nothing supernatural (though, who knows, maybe the moon goddess Hecate turned against the Cardinals).

The eclipse had been previously scheduled. It was poetic, and so part of the story, the myth now told.

Red Sox fans make great claims for "The Steal" and their World Series victory. "There is just no better story in the history of sports." "It is the greatest story ever told." Such hyperbole is understandable. Victory. Happiness. "The Steal" marked a new beginning, but this story is only new for the Red Sox. It is actually a very old story. I contemplated this, among other things, as I put my sleeping daughter to bed that evening. I have contemplated it ever since. This is why "The Steal" means so much to me.

In addition to the crucial turn "The Steal" gave to the story of the series, a larger meaning to the moment was felt by everyone watching. This intuition persists in the chills I feel now recalling it. In this revelatory moment, the greater spiritual significance of the game itself can be felt. Spirits rise and fall, and so goes success and happiness.

He seized the day. "The Steal": the right place and the right time, the right person, picked up for the postseason for just such a moment, does the right thing. In fact, before the next season, Roberts is traded away. But when he visits Boston again, even while wearing the uniform of another team, the fans at Fenway stand and applaud. Everyone knows: happiness began with "The Steal." This is the crux of all of our efforts—that when we do our best, our best will be good enough to make the crucial difference. Our efforts so often wait for affirmation. Too often virtue is only its own reward. Too often it is only how you play the game that matters, not whether you win or lose. But happiness eludes us as long as victory eludes us.

When I recall "The Steal," when I try to describe the moment, I shudder. Something so natural, so human, the running figure— nothing else like it in the animal kingdom (running upright is as much in our nature as is reasoning). It invites contemplation. I see the man run faster, as if the earth had tilted to help him accelerate downhill, as if time slowed for a moment to allow his reaching fingers to sneak beneath the shortstop Derek Jeter's swiping glove. My imagination offers up "as ifs." I need metaphors to recapture the moment, to carry my own spirit and evoke again the elation I felt. Coaches speak of "motivation" as if athletes were actors. Analysts speak of "momentum" as if physics, Newton's laws of motion, could describe the superfluid fluctuations, the complex and creative evolutions of our psyches.

I did not always see so much in the game of baseball. But when I reflected upon "The Steal," wistfully and with envy as a Cubs fan, I knew enough to see in it a distillation of the ancient wisdom of which baseball is a repository.

HOW TO LIVE

"The Steal" is the answer. This is how you want to live. When the moment comes along, you want to make that one move, that one gesture that will make everything else fall into place.

"The Steal" was the pivotal moment in the myth of the Red Sox victory. The word "myth" comes from the Greek word *mythos*, which simply means story. For rationalists, myths are just that, just a story. Today to say something is a "myth" is to say that it is not true. But when I say that baseball is a myth, I mean that each ball game enacts a story that reverberates in the psyche. It is a pleasing story. It is also a story with a lesson, a life lesson. A story about a hero coming home. Baseball reveals the *telos*, the purpose, the aim, or as they say, "the meaning" of life. And baseball is the myth America tells itself about excellence and success, or as the ancients say, virtue and victory—about happiness. The pursuit of excellence, baseball teaches, is the best pursuit of happiness.

Q: Did I raise Cecilia a Cubs fan?

A: Yes, and no.

Yes, all through her teenage years, we still spent hot summer days and stormy autumn nights together at the ballpark, eating hot dogs and talking. And even now that she's grown up, graduated from college and moved to New York City to pursue her career, she still cheers for the Cubs from afar.

But no, she's not a baseball fanatic, not like me. The game does not provide the central myths through which she contemplates her life. The little girl I once dressed all in Cubby blue is now a devotee of high fashion, art, and design. She exhibits the courage to dress for herself, which is often pretty avant-garde. She possesses the prudence to suit her style to the company and the occasion. She exercises—or tries her best to exercise—temperance before buying another new pair of shoes. "But, Dad, they're so beautiful! Or are they sublime?" The ancient wisdom I rediscovered with her at the game, she has found her own way, given her own passions and interests, to apply to her own life. She's living her own myth, of which she is a hero in pursuit of her own particular happiness.

....

Note: I had thought I would be happy when the Red Sox won, and I was, to an extent. But my immediate thought was, "I wish it was the Cubs."

For me, the story of "The Steal" (a play worthy of cunning, courageous Odysseus), the story of the Red Sox World Series victory after eighty-six years, was also the story that told me I was a Cubs fan. From the perspective of the Cubs fan, I looked on from without, with envy and wistfulness. I understood the ancient equation between excellence, fortune, success, and happiness. I understood it, but I didn't fully feel it. Not yet. Ancient wisdom teaches that happiness is something extra, that happiness comes when you do everything the right way and you're lucky, i.e., the ball bounces your way. For my Cubs, all curses aside, virtue had as yet only been its own reward. The goddess Fortuna had not smiled upon the North Side of Chicago. Not yet.

HAPPINESS

Cubs Win!

The Chicago Cubs are World Series Champions!

I stand outside of myself, ecstatic, gawking at the TV screen. My kids run in circles around the living room, their arms in the air, screaming. Cats scurry for cover. The dog is suddenly on his feet, barking alarm. My wife points beyond the "W" flag now hanging on our living room window, where outside the night sky pulsates, lighting up from fireworks not three miles away exploding over Wrigley Field. Car horns blare, and shouts rise up from the street below, then comes the delayed thunder of the fireworks. It seems right that my senses are discombobulated. On TV, players pop champagne. I pop champagne on my side of the screen too. Bubbles running over, I am already dizzy. Highlights of the game begin replaying. We stare and cheer all over again, clapping, hollering, shaking our heads.

How to make sense of it, the Cubs, World Series Champions?!

HOW THIS FEELS

Before the game started, I was startled to hear Pete Rose say that this—Game 7 of the 2016 World Series—was the biggest ball game of his lifetime. Was it simply the history, the textbook fact that the Cubs had not won since 1908?

Afterward I am amazed to hear expert analysts refer to Game 7 as one of the greatest ball games ever played. I consider myself a student of the game but confess that at first, I cannot judge. I heard team owner Tom Ricketts describe being similarly over-whelmed by the Series: "It was the nine best days of my life, and I can't remember any of it."

Now that the Cubs have won, I am giddy, elated, confused with euphoria, befuddled by joy. I am not relieved. Let me be clear. Eleven days before, when the Cubs won the National League Pennant at Wrigley, then I was relieved. There in the stands at Wrigley, my own cry of triumph (with Cecilia screaming beside me) had been one with the crashing tidal wave roar of the crowd. We all shared in a communal catharsis: our souls cleansed by suc-cess, we looked forward to our team playing in the World Series for the first time since 1945.

Fast-forward now to the final play of that Series replaying on my television and behold: third baseman Kris Bryant, already smiling, charges the infield grounder, scoops it up smoothly (as is his way), and steps to throw but slips on the wet grass (which was the way of this game of twists and turns), yet still slings it sharply across the diamond into first baseman Anthony Rizzo's waiting mitt. That final play of this Game 7 expresses perfectly what I'd felt: rising hope, apprehension, then disoriented joy!

When I fall asleep that night, I feel like I must already be dreaming. Yet when I wake up the next morning, it is still true. There is an empty champagne bottle on the windowsill. My head aches. I smile. It has happened. The Cubs have won the World Series! What does it mean?

I have been contemplating the meaning of baseball for years.

I have cultivated a connoisseurship of the game and indulged in a fanatical passion for the Cubs. I have given baseball the same quality of attention that priests give to scripture, that Buddhist monks give to sutras, that the ancient philosophers gave to Homer's epic poems. I have discerned an ancient wisdom in the motions of the action on the field. I have found in the game a guide to recovering the classic way to happiness. Yet now my happy feelings eclipse my thinking. The Cubs' victory has rendered everything relative. Having just witnessed it with my own eyes, I cannot really believe it, nor can I say how I feel. I feel too much. I remember Kris Bryant struggling to formulate the paradoxical experience: "I mean, I'm out here crying, man. I'm so happy. I can't really put into words how this feels."[1]

WHAT HAPPENED

When seeing is no longer believing and emotion defies expression, it may be better (before trying to say what it all means) to revisit, if only to savor, what actually happened.

The 2016 Chicago Cubs, after leading Major League Baseball in wins from Opening Day until the close of the regular season, after defeating the Giants in a five-game series and Los Angeles in seven, won the National League Pennant. In the World Series, after going down to the Cleveland Indians three games to one, the Cubs battled back to force a deciding Game 7. It is November (the 2nd, a Wednesday), and somehow we're all still watching baseball! Over forty thousand fans gather in and around Cleveland's Progressive Field, over forty million sit in front of their TV sets at home. Among these witnesses, I am one.

The Cubs and the Indians, now tied three games apiece, have both proved their excellence. Neither team has taken more than one game at home. This series has had everything: rising rookies, seasoned veterans, dominating aces, crafty relievers, clutch hitting, home runs, stolen bases, acrobatic defense, stories within stories, a week and a half of suspenseful soap-operatic action. Game 7 will have all this also, with the drama overflowing nine innings into extra play.

Starting for the Indians is their ace Corey Kluber, who thus far in the series has stymied Cubs hitters with a sinker, a hard slider, and a wicked, diving curve. In two games, he has pitched twelve innings, allowing only one run. Tonight, though, is his third start in nine days. This will be the third chance for our hitters to see the ball out of his hand, and his arm has got to be tired. I keep telling myself that it's got to be.

Kluber throws a strike and then two balls. The next pitch he puts over the plate, our lead-off man Dexter Fowler drives high into center. When it sails over the wall, Fowler, already at first, turns in disbelief to his teammates, who look back at him bug-eyed from the dugout. Fowler actually runs backward for a few strides toward second, smiling widely.

"He has a great smile," says my wife. So she says every time she sees Fowler. I cannot disagree. With no outs in the 1st, we are already up 1–0!

Our starter is Kyle Hendricks, a youngster. Out of spring training, he had to win a place in the rotation. He played college ball at Dartmouth so, of course, his teammates call him "The Professor." You don't have to be a professor to understand that his regular-season 2.13 ERA was the best in all of baseball. His fastball never gets out of the eighties. Rather than throw harder, Hendricks throws smarter. His pitch selection has the misdirection of a magician. His command is perfection. In the 1st, he does not give up a hit. In the 2nd, he lets an Indian on but immediately picks him off at first. When a second Indian gets on, he induces a double play to get out of the inning. The canny Ivy Leaguer can strike you out swinging or induce you to exercise his defense. In the 3rd, however, Hendricks allows a couple of hits, and the Indians tie it, 1–1.

Leading off for us in the 4th, Kris Bryant works himself into a full count against Kluber before shooting one through the heart of the infield for a base hit. Bryant goes to second when Anthony Rizzo (who likes to crowd the plate) is hit by a pitch. Ben Zobrist grounds into a fielder's choice to put Bryant on third. Then Addison Russell pops one up that seems too shallow for a sacrifice. Indians outfielder Rajai Davis must think so too because he hesitates for a heartbeat while Bryant tags at third. Bryant is tall, faster than he looks, and takes long strides. He slides between the catcher's legs, stretching his toe to the plate beneath the tag. Safe! The Cubs regain the lead 2–1!

"This is the Cubs," I pronounce, leaning forward. All year this team has manufactured runs, the entire lineup contributing. When next our rookie catcher Willson Contreras bounces one off the center field wall, driving in Zobrist, I simply nod in emphatic agreement with myself. 3–1.

In the top of the 5th, Javy Báez cranks one over the wall in right center—it's 4–1!—and so drives the heretofore indomitable Kluber out of the game after just fifty-seven pitches. Next in for the Indians is their tall, lanky super reliever, Andrew Miller. Miller's array of pitches originate from the obscure outskirts of his windup to feather the farthest corners of the plate. Few Cubs have been able to get a bead on him, much less hit him squarely all series long. But Bryant stares him down for a walk, and Rizzo drives him in. 5–1!

This is the Cubs! Hey, hey! For the first four and a half

innings, the story has been a happy ensemble performance with Hendricks's prudent pitching and our lineup all working together to build a solid lead. While Indians fans grimace, Cubs fans wear grins, the classic mask of comedy.

PLOT TWISTS

The next four and a half innings, however, tell another story. It is a goat song, a tragedy. Though in the bottom of the 5th Hendricks continues to look good, sitting down the first two batters in the inning, the umpire loses his concentration, makes some bad calls, and gifts an Indian a base on balls. Our manager Joe Maddon loses his nerve and decides to bring in our multimillion-dollar certified ace Jon Lester. I try to rationalize, "Lester won the World Series twice with the Red Sox. Lester's lifetime postseason ERA is 2.51." I'm reciting this litany in order to reassure myself of Maddon's wisdom, but I am not so sure.

"What is Maddon doing?" My wife looks at me accusingly. I admire Maddon as a modern-day philosopher king. She says, "He's overthinking us out of a victory!"

Sure enough, Lester immediately gives up a cheap bouncer in front of the plate to Jason Kipnis.

"Kipnis!" my wife hisses. The affable Chicago native and confessed childhood Cubs fan has been killing us all series long. Now the Tribe has runners on second and third. Lester throws a wild pitch in the dirt that careens off catcher David Ross's face mask, knocking him onto his rear end. Looking like the old man, the "Grandpa" he and his teammates have joked about all season long, Ross has fallen and can't get up, and by the time he does, two runs have scored. It's now 5–3.

In the 6th, however, Ross gets a run back by driving one off

Miller over the center field wall. Ross is expressionless as he runs around the bases. I wonder if he's concussed from taking one off the forehead in the previous inning. Back in the dugout, Ross observes, "I just went deep in Game 7 of the World Series." Indeed. It's 6–3![2]

Lester gets the Cubs through seven and two-thirds innings, looking strong after his disastrous first few pitches. But when a hit that our shortstop can't handle puts an Indian on first, Maddon calls for his closer Aroldis Chapman. My wife puts her hands on her head, continuing in her role as Cassandra: "Chapman has to be tired!"

I first saw Chapman at Wrigley a year earlier. He was then pitching for the Cincinnati Reds. I took a picture of the radar gun reading on the big screen: 103 mph! I had never seen such a feat. It was reported that he had thrown as hard as 105. Yet Chapman was a controversial acquisition for the Cubs. He was suspended by his previous team earlier in the summer for a domestic assault allegation. Apparently he and his wife had a heated argument wherein he brandished a gun and shot up his drum set while she called the cops. Now in Chicago, he was surly with the local press when asked about the incident. On the field, however, he was a cool cat. Strolling nonchalantly to the mound to blaring hard rock, draping his arm around his catcher's shoulders while casually conferring, he presented the picture of composure, control, and bat-breaking, head-shaking, terrifying, crowd-rousing velocity. His nickname is the "Cuban Missile," but he is a smart weapon. He varies speeds, trajectories, and locations. His off-speed pitches are the speed of most fastballs. At Wrigley Field in Game 5 of the World Series, I witnessed him get eight outs for us. He shut down the Indians and personally sent the series back to Cleveland. Maddon used him again to close out Game 6. Now he is called into Game 7. The Cubs are here playing today, thanks to Chapman. Yet it is Chapman who will give it up.

Indian Brandon Guyer works the count full, then doubles, driving in a run. 6–4.

Now Rajai Davis courageously crouches in the box, fouling off fastballs. With a two-two count, Davis chokes up on his bat, desperately flailing to stay alive. Chapman fires one ankle high that Davis reaches down for and somehow connects with. It doesn't seem hard hit, nor does it look like it'll stay fair, but then, just inside the left field pole, it flies over the wall. What? A home run?!

Tie game, 6–6. Pandemonium at Progressive Field. Back home in Chicago? Nausea. Vertigo.

A stunned Chapman somehow gets out of the inning. Though the Cubs threaten in the 9th, trying to manufacture a go-ahead run, Cleveland's young shortstop Francisco Lindor makes a great play to strand our runner at third.

In the bottom of the 9th, with the game still tied, our all-of-a-sudden humbled, all-too-human Chapman is tossing in off-speed stuff in the low nineties and high eighties. He's relying on the Indians to provide high-flying fouls for strikes and pop-ups for loud outs. He and the Cubs survive the 9th. Back in the dugout, Chapman is inconsolable. Tears stream down his cheeks. And with these grown man's tears, down comes the rain. A deluge off Lake Erie consumes Cleveland. The grounds crew hurries to roll out the tarp. The game must be delayed before extra innings may be played.

HOPE FLICKERS

I take the dog outside for a walk around the block. Everything the Cubs did has been undone by these Indians. In Chicago, it's not raining, but it's damp. Cool mist makes the street gleam with a ghostly aura. I seem to be the only one outside. The windows in the multistory facades of the block flicker with the haunting blue light of TV screens. The streets are as empty as I now feel.

The dog pees, pulls on his leash to go explore the neighborhood, but I can barely put one foot in front of the other. I am numb. Dread rises in my throat, choking out hope. "Damn it," I say aloud and lead the dog back inside to face whatever will happen next.

On TV, the tarp is being peeled off the field. The game, the series, the season will now come down to one inning.

THE PLAY WITHIN THE PLAY

Both closers are out. The Cubs are up first and in higher spirits than me. (We will learn later that right fielder #22 Jason Heyward used the rain delay to rouse his teammates with a stirring speech reminding them of their virtue and that victory was yet at hand.) Our young designated hitter, Kyle Schwarber, strokes one into right. On first, he pumps his fist, calling to his teammates in the dugout, "Here we go!" Speedy rookie Albert Almora Jr. comes in to run. Next up is Bryant, who drives one deep—stand up, hold your breath—onto the warning track, where it's caught. But Almora, prudent beyond his years, has the wherewithal to tag and take second. (These kids know how to play.) Thinking to set up a double play, the Indians walk Rizzo. But Zobrist, up next, foils their plan, shooting the ball just beyond the outstretched glove of the diving third baseman into the left field corner for a double. Almora claps his hands as he steps on home. The camera flashes to Zobrist stomping on the second-base bag with both cleats, roaring like an ancient warrior, shaking his helmet askew.

On third, wide-eyed Rizzo pulls his helmet over his ears as if to keep from losing his mind. The Cubs lead 7–6!

Pinch-hitting Miguel Montero drives in Rizzo. 8–6! Then with the bases loaded Indians Game 5 starter Trevor Bauer comes in to get out our next two batters, keeping Cleveland within striking distance.

And, of course, in the bottom of the 10th, the Indians mount a rally. Our pitcher gets two out, but then Guyer—again, Guyer!—walks on. And Davis—again, Davis!—gets a hit, driving in Guyer. Like a recurring nightmare, like a play within a play, the Cubs have gone up and so the Indians are coming back: it's 8–7!

Who knows how long extra innings will last? Will the rain return to delay play? Emotion renders time relative. The minutes elapse sporadically with the speed of a pitch and the swing of a bat. The seconds lag with how long it takes to tag up, and then accelerate as a runner sprints to the next base. We count the moments with shouts and sighs. It is an old chestnut that baseball is untimed and so any game might never end, but this Game 7 feels like proof of that philosophical fancy.

Then Maddon brings in young lefty Mike Montgomery. His looping lollipop curveball at 77 mph elicits from the Indians' switch-hitting utility man a bouncing grounder. Here comes a hard-charging, already-grinning Bryant to glove the ball and throw it to Rizzo. Cubs win! Cubs win! Cubs win!

WHAT IT MEANS

The next day, fire trucks create a light and water show around the Cubs' jet plane as it taxies at O'Hare. The day after, the City of Chicago holds a parade to honor its team. On top of double-decker buses, the players ride from Wrigley Field to Lake

Shore Drive, then down the Magnificent Mile to Grant Park. Along the route and in the park are five million fans, my family among them. It is one of the largest gatherings of human beings in recorded history. Other such gatherings were along sacred rivers in India, holy pilgrimages in Iraq, the funeral of the Ayatollah Khomeini, and the Pope saying Mass in Manila.

The Cubs parade is a sacred occasion of sorts. People gather to express their gratitude and share their joy. Long-deferred hopes have at last been fulfilled. Whereas usual religious gatherings are expressions of faith, at this parade, I think, we are trying to dispel our disbelief. People hold up signs and repeat the phrase: "It Happened." We are trying to convince ourselves that this incredible event, which we have all witnessed for ourselves, actually occurred. "It's unbelievable," Bryant says of the parade. "It's probably the coolest thing I've been a part of. I think it's even cooler than winning the World Series. Just seeing all these people come out. They've waited a long time for this moment. I have no words."[3]

Reporters poll the crowd, trying to find the words. "Can you believe it?" "What does this mean to you?" Even as we come to credit the truth of our victory, we still ask, what does it mean?

EPIC

This is the word most used to describe the Cubs' World Series win. Epic. Especially its last game, with its vast cast of contributing characters, its changes in momentum and mood, its deus ex machina rain delay, and its "Mousetrap" of an extra inning. World Series MVP Ben Zobrist, who ripped the go-ahead RBI in the 10th, said, "It was just an epic battle."[4]

"Epic" from the Greek simply means "a word, a song, a story."

In his *Poetics*, Aristotle describes an epic as a long narrative.[5] "Epic" might just mean long. (It certainly seemed like a long time since the Cubs won the Pennant, like an eternity since they clinched the Division.) Yet when you see the stories the philosophers are talking about, you realize that epics encompass everything.

Epics are religious, not just because they depict gods and heroes, but in the root sense of the word. "Religion" is from Latin "*re-ligare*," meaning to relink together. (It is the same ligare as in "ligament," as in Kyle Schwarber tore a ligament in his knee during the third game of the regular season yet was able to come back to play in the World Series.) Epics connect seemingly disparate elements into a meaningful whole and so offer a vision of the world.

Seven ball games, of course, do not contain gods or war or hell or heaven or elves or dragons. Yet I nod when I hear the word "epic" applied to the Cubs' win. Zobrist stomping and screaming after his go-ahead run-scoring double in the 10th is a berserker out of Beowulf or, better, from Homer's *Iliad*, a battle-ravished Ajax venting his heroic fury to the sky. The 2016 World Series, with its episodic ups and downs, its heroes and its goats, the virtues displayed as well as the errors made, distilled and dramatized the values baseball embodies. The Cubs winning is a revelation of the ancient wisdom of baseball. Its story traces the connection between virtue, fortune, victory, and happiness. The Cubs winning, this strange happiness—that it happened, they won!—is a revelation of how things mean at all. Meaning is situational, contextual, connectional, communal. Meaning, put simply, implies a "world." Recounting this 2016 World Series, I feel an electric connection—is that you, Zeus?—between ancient Greece and modern America, between Homer's heroes and my Cubbies. Did I raise Cecilia a Cubs fan? When the Cubs won, she confesses, it was something akin to rapture.

After my family and I return home from the parade, I turn on the TV, still happily asking, what does it mean? The best answer I hear comes from an old grandmother conducting her entire clan of blue-clad Cubs fans, her children and her grandchildren, from the parade. When asked the question, she bursts out both in laughter and in tears: "What does it mean? It means everything. *Que significa todo el mundo para mi*. It means the world to me."

NOTES

PREGAME

1. This photograph was obtained from the digital collection of the New York Public Library. The creator and copyright status are unknown.

2. The myth of the sphinx, older than historical record, was known across the Mediterranean world. The most famous telling in Greek is Sophocles' tragedy *Oedipus the King* (fifth century BCE), where the hero meets the fantastic beast outside Thebes. In Egypt the famous statue of the Great Sphinx of Giza (twenty-sixth century BCE) may be male. Like a gargoyle above the door of a Gothic cathedral, images of a sphinx can ward away evil.

1ST INNING

1. I first read the *Odyssey* during high school in Robert Fitzgerald's translation (1961). In college I studied Richard Lattimore's translation (1965). Robert Fagles's translation (1996) traveled with baby Cecilia in her perambulator when I was teaching in the University of Chicago's "Great Books" program. Today I also rely, for instruction and pleasure, on the translations of Stanley Lombardo (2000), Samuel Butler (1900), and Alexander Pope (1725). For the Greek and facing translation see the Loeb edition in two volumes by George E. Dimock and A. T. Murray (Cambridge: Harvard, 1995).

2. Homer, *Odyssey*, Robert Fagles trans. (New York: Viking, 1996), 24.210.

3. Bob Carter, "Hustle Made Rose Respected, Infamous," ESPN.com, https://www.espn.com/sportscentury/features/00016443.html.

2ND INNING

1. Euclid, *Elements*, Book XI, Definition 14, David E. Joyce trans., https://www.mlb.com/video/reliving-the-moment-ichiro-broke-the-hit-record?q=Ichiro&cp=CMS_FIRST&qt=FREETEXT&p=0.

2. "Euclid's Elements of Geometry Fleuron N007820-57," Wikimedia Commons, accessed August 23, 2024, https://www.mlb.com/video/reliving-the-moment-ichiro-broke-the-hit-record?q=Ichiro&cp=CMS_FIRST&qt=FREETEXT&p=0.

3. "BB Moments: Willie Mays's Catch," MLB.com Film Room, September 29, 1954, 2:59, https://www.mlb.com/video/bb-moments-willie-mays-catch-c3218956.

4. Arnold Hano, *A Day in the Bleachers* (Cambridge: DaCapo Press, 1995), 123–24.

5. Hano, *Bleachers*, 124.

6. "Relive Ichiro's Legendary Throw from Right Field," MLB Film Room, May 26, 2024, 0:33, https://www.mlb.com/video/relieve-ichiro-s-legendary-throw-from-right-field.

7. David Shields, "Being Ichiro," *The New York Times Magazine*, September 16, 2001, https://www.nytimes.com/2001/09/16/magazine/being-ichiro.html/.

8. Robert Whiting, *The Meaning of Ichiro* (New York: Warner Books, 2004), 29.

9. Homer, *Odyssey*, Samuel Butler trans. (1900), 9.21–22.

3RD INNING

1. A pithy definition often quoted but without certain citation. An early—perhaps the earliest in print—attribution is in poet Donald Hall's review of Robert E. Hood's *The Gashouse Gang* (1976): Donald Hall, "The Gashouse Gang," *The New York Times*, May 9, 1976, https://www.nytimes.com/1976/05/09/archives/the-gashouse-gang.html/.

2. For the *Iliad* I rely on translations by Stanley Lombardo (1997), Robert Fagles (1990), Richard Lattimore (1951), and Alexander Pope (1720). Also see Christopher Logue's extraordinary rendering *War Music: An Account of Homer's Iliad* (New York: Farrar, Straus & Giroux, 2015). For a wonderful survey of how Homer has been translated into English, see George Steiner's *Homer in English* (New York: Penguin, 1996). Also see Eva Brann's delightful and deeply insightful *Homeric Moments* (Philadelphia: Paul Dry, 2002).

3. Homer, *Iliad*, 22.

4. Richard Ben Cramer, *Joe DiMaggio: The Hero's Life* (New York: Touchstone, 2000), 360.

5. Bill Chastain and Jesse Rogers, *Try Not to Suck: The Extraordinary Baseball Life of Joe Maddon* (Chicago: Triumph, 2018).

6. Ted Williams and John Underwood, *The Science of Hitting* (New York: Fireside, 1970), 7.

7. Philip Hersh, "Kris Bryant's Remarkable Connection with his Dad—and Ted Williams," *The Chicago Tribune*, August 23, 2019, https://www.chicagotribune.com/2015/09/08/kris-bryants-remarkable-connection-with-his-dad-and-with-ted-williams/.

8. Homer, *Iliad*, Stanley Lombardo trans. (Indianapolis: Hackett, 1997), 1.2-6.

9. Ken Burns dir., "The National Pastime," Episode 6 of *Baseball*, PBS, 28:45–50. On Williams's anger, also see Richard Ben Cramer, *What Do You Think of Ted Williams Now? A Remembrance* (New York: Simon and Schuster, 2002).

10. Hersh, "Kris Bryant's Remarkable Connection."

11. Gordon Wittenmyer, "Curtain Call on the Road? 'I'm Not That Guy,' Says Kris Bryant," *Chicago Sun-Times*, June 28, 2016, https://chicago.suntimes .com/2016/6/28/18345850/curtain-call-on-the-road-i-m-not-that-guy -says-kris-bryant/.

12. Hersh, "Kris Bryant's Remarkable Connection."

13. Ben Cosman, "Kris Bryant Made the Final Out of Game 7, Smiling the Entire Time," November 3, 2016, https://www.mlb.com/cut4/ kris-bryant-smiled-while-he-made-final-out-of-world-series-c207986770/.

14. Jackie Robinson, *I Never Had It Made* (New York: Ecco, 1995), 28.

15. Robinson, *Made*, 42.

16. Robinson, *Made*, 31–33.

17. Martin Luther King Jr., "I Have a Dream," August 28, 1963, https:// www.archives.gov/files/social-media/transcripts/transcript-march- pt3-of-3-2602934.pdf/.

18. Mike Bertha, "Martin Luther King Jr. and Jackie Robinson: Friends and Civil Rights Icons," MLB.com, January 18, 2016, https://www.mlb.com/cut4/ mlk-jr-and-jackie-robinson-were-good-friends-c162102154/.

19. Recreated figure based on "Jackie Robinson's Retired Number 42.sv," Wikimedia Commons, accessed August 23, 2024, https://commons. wikimedia.org/wiki/File:Jackie_Robinson%27s_retired_number_42.svg. "We'll all wear #42" exclaimed by Robinson's Dodger teammate Gene Hermanski as reported by Vin Scully. Andrew Mearns, "Listen to Vin Scully Tell One of His Very Favorite Stories About Jackie Robinson and the No. 42," Cut4, April 16, 2017, https://www.mlb.com/cut4/ vin-scully-recounts-jackie-robinson-day-story-of-number-42-c224629020.

4TH INNING

1. Plutarch (first century CE) says: "Most authors tell the story that Alexander finding himself unable to untie the knot, the ends of which were secretly twisted round and folded up within it, cut it asunder with his sword. But Aristobulus tells us it was easy for him to undo it, by only pulling the pin out of the pole, to which the yoke was tied, and afterwards drawing off the yoke itself from below." Whether one sides with "most authors" or with Aristobulus may depend upon whether one wishes Alexander's legendary unknotting to exemplify courage or prudence. Plutarch, "Alexander," *Lives*, Arthur Hugh Clough ed. (1859), John Dryden trans. (1683), Volume II (New York: Modern Library, 1992), 152.

2. Aristotle, *Nicomachean Ethics*, Joe Sachs trans. (Indianapolis: Focus, 2002), 6:11.

3. Christy Mathewson, *Pitching in a Pinch* (Lincoln, Nebraska: Bison, 1994), 13.

4. Randy Voorhees and Mark Gola, *As Koufax Said . . . : The 400 Greatest Things Ever Said About How to Play Baseball* (New York: Contemporary Books, 2003), 66.

5. Mathewson, *Pitching*, 19.

6. Mathewson, *Pitching*, 21.

7. Mathewson, *Pitching*, 35.

8. Mathewson, *Pitching*, 19.

9. Mathewson, *Pitching*, 36.

10. Mathewson, *Pitching*, 57.

5TH INNING

1. William Blake, "I Want! I Want!" engraving, 1793.

2. Walt Whitman, *Leaves of Grass* (1855).

3. Sigmund Freud, *Civilization and Its Discontents* (1930).

4. Stanley Kubrick dir., *Doctor Strangelove*, 1964, Columbia Pictures.

5. Herbert Ross dir., *Play It Again, Sam*, 1972, Paramount Pictures.

6. Homer, *Odyssey*, Robert Fagles trans., 9.438–40.

7. "My ash spear is my barley bread. / My ash spear is my Ismarian wine. / I lean on my spear and drink." Guy Davenport trans., *7 Greeks* (New York: New Directions, 1995), 23.

8. "Piniella's Ejection," MLB.com Film Room, June 2, 2007, https://www.mlb.com/video/piniella-s-ejection-c20046317/.

6TH INNING

1. Plato, *Republic*, with interpretive essay by Allan Bloom trans. (New York: Basic Books, 1968).

2. William James, "The Moral Equivalent of War," Lecture 11 in *Memories and Studies* (New York: Longmans, Green, and Co., 1911).

3. Sophocles, "Ajax"; Homer, *Odyssey*, 11.

4. Johan Huizinga, *Homo Ludens: A Study of the Play Element in Culture* (Boston: Beacon Press, 1955), 11–12.

5. Homer, *Iliad*, 18.

6. "1720 image from THE ILLIAD OF HOMER (translated by POPE) pg 171 Vol 5 The Shield of Achilles.png," Wikimedia Commons, accessed August 23, 2024, https://commons.wikimedia.org/wiki/File:1720_image_from_THE_ILLIAD_OF_HOMER_(translated_by_POPE)_pg_171_Vol_5_The_Shield_of_Achilles.png.

TOP OF THE 7TH

1. Walt Whitman, *Leaves of Grass* (1855).

7TH INNING STRETCH

1. Homer, *Odyssey*, Robert Fagles trans., 8, 538–40.

BOTTOM OF THE 7TH

1. William Shakespeare, *King Lear*, Act III, scene i.

2. Longinus, Penelope Murray and T. S. Dorsch trans., "On the Sublime," Chapter 35 in *Classical Literary Criticism* (New York: Penguin, 2001), 155.

3. James Ivory dir., *Howards End*, 1992, Sony Pictures Classics. Savor the line as delivered in Merchant and Ivory's 1992 film.

4. Robert W. Creamer, *Babe: The Legend Comes to Life* (New York: Fireside, 1974), 367.

8TH INNING

1. John Boardman et al., *The Oxford History of the Classical World: The Roman World* (Oxford: Oxford University Press, 1986), 151.

2. William James, *A Pluralistic Universe* (New York: Longmans, Green, and Co., 1909), 299–300.

3. Jack Curry, "Principles Keep Father From Seeing Alou Play," *The New York Times*, September 24, 2007, https://www.nytimes.com/2007/09/24/sports/baseball/24alou.html/.

4. Mark 15:34 and Matthew 27:46, *King James Bible*.

5. "Statement From Cubs Fan Steve Bartman," Associated Press, October 15, 2003, https://www.foxnews.com/story/statement-from-cubs-fan-steve-bartman/.

6. Leviticus 16:10, *King James Bible*.

7. Jonathan Alter, "The Reason for the Cubs Fiasco," *Newsweek*, Oct 27, 2003, 54.

8. "The Billy Goat Curse," Billy Goat Tavern and Grill, https://www.billygoattavern.com/legend/curse/.

9TH INNING

1. Jack Curry, "Baseball: With 400 Saves, a One-Pitch Wonder Heads for Hall of Fame," *The New York Times*, July 16, 2006, https://www.nytimes.com/2006/07/17/sports/17iht-base.2218900.html/.

2. Craig Calcaterra, "Mariano Rivera's Cutter: 'A Gift from God,'" NBC Sports, March 2, 2012, https://www.nbcsports.com/mlb/news/mariano-riveras-cutter-a-gift-from-god/.

3. *Tito: The Terry Francona Story*, MLB Network Presents documentary, 2023.

4. Ian Browne, "Genius Moniker: Origin of '04 Sox 'Idiots,'" MLB.com, February 5, 2021, https://www.mlb.com/news/2004-red-sox-idiots-nickname-explained/.

5. "BB Moments: Reverse The Curse," Red Sox @ Yankees, MLB Film Room, October 20, 2004, https://www.mlb.com/video/bb-moments-reverse-the-curse-c3218904/.

EXTRA INNING

1. Ben Cosman, "Kris Bryant Made the Final Out of Game 7, Smiling the Entire Time," November 3, 2016, https://www.mlb.com/cut4/kris-bryant-smiled-while-he-made-final-out-of-world-series-c207986770/.

2. Jed Tuminaro dir., *The 2016 World Series*, MLB Productions, 2016.

3. "Chicago Cubs Kris Bryant and David Ross Celebrate with Ellen!" YouTube, November 9, 2016, 4:41, https://www.youtube.com/watch?v=ipFq3Gc5XGU/.

4. Steve Keating, "Zobrist Named World Series MVP," Reuters, November 3, 2016, https://www.reuters.com/article/sports/zobrist-named-world-series-mvp-idUSKBN12Y0AS/#.

5. Aristotle, *Poetics*, 23–24.

ACKNOWLEDGMENTS

I am grateful to Tanya Hall, Brian Welch, and everyone at Greenleaf Book Group—thank you, Chase Quarterman, for a cover I love!—but I am especially grateful to my editor, Lee Reed Zarnikau, for her thoughtful, insightful, and always tactful guidance. Thanks, Beowulf Sheehan, for a fantastic author photo! Thank you, Luke Jermay, for your wise guidance. Thank you so much, Robert Cocuzzo, for all your help and encouragement!

I am thankful to everyone who has sat beside me at Wrigley Field over the years, from my cousin Tom McMillian to my friends and teachers from the University of Chicago—including Michael Kessler, Jean-Luc Marion, and Steve Peterson. I am especially thankful for epic conversations with Michael and Peter O'Leary, even though they root for the White Sox.

I've spent the most time at the ball game with my family. My mother took me to Little League practice and cheered for me from behind the backstop. My father and my grandfather took me to Fenway often as a boy. I've spent countless happy days and evenings at Wrigley Field with Cecilia and also with my son, Thomas (who has gone to the game with me more than anyone). I owe the greatest debt of gratitude to my wife, who has always been my closest confidant, my best critic, and my most loyal and encouraging fan. Thank you, Hille.

Go Cubs!

ABOUT THE AUTHOR

Author photograph by Beowulf Sheehan

CHRISTIAN SHEPPARD'S essays on religion, culture, and sports have appeared in *The New York Times*, *Chicago Tribune*, and *The Journal of Religion*, among other publications. He has lectured at the Chicago Cultural Center, Chicago Shakespeare Theatre, and the Baseball Hall of Fame. He is co-editor of *Mystics: Presence and Aporia* (University of Chicago Press). For a decade, he taught the "Great Books" at the University of Chicago and presently teaches Liberal Arts at the School of the Art Institute of Chicago. He lives within walking distance of Wrigley Field.